"It's no surprise that Stephanie has compiled THE book of outcome-oriented, clean recipes designed for athletic performance. With over 20 years of success as a sports competitor in her rearview mirror, she shows all of us how to push to the next level while supporting genuine recovery utilizing the oldest and most reliable product on the market: whole, pure food. Victory has never tasted so good."

—CIARRA HANNAH, author of *The Frugal Paleo Cookbook*

"There is a lot of confusion on when and what to eat to optimize health and performance. Not only does this book have delectable food ideas, but it also clarifies when to eat them!"

—EVA TWARDOKENS, Two-time Olympian in Alpine Skiing, Class of 2011 Ski Hall of Fame

"Finally, a nutrition resource for those who are looking to improve their performance that does not rely on gimmicks, fads or a myriad of supplements. Easy-to-make recipes based on the science of performance nutrition from an individual who is an athlete in her own right—we are sold."

—DR. ANASTASIA BOULAIS AND JAIME SCOTT, Cofounders of the Ancestral Health Society of New Zealand

"Finally, a Paleo cookbook for strength athletes, written by a strength athlete. We all know the Paleo diet produces fantastic results for the everyday Joe and Jane, but can Paleo improve the performance of those looking to jump higher, move faster and hoist heavier weights? Absolutely. And in *The Performance Paleo Cookbook*, Stephanie Gaudreau will show you how to do just that."

—KEITH NORRIS, Cofounder of PaleoFX and Founder of Ancestral Momentum

PAGE STREET
PUBLISHING CO.

First published in 2015 by

Page Street Publishing Co.

27 Congress Street, Suite 103

Salem, MA 01970

www.pagestreetpublishing.com

Distributed by Macmillan; sales in Canada by The Canadian Manda Group; distribution in Canada by The Jaguar Book Group.

18   17   16   15   4 5

ISBN-13: 978-1-62414-101-0

ISBN-10: 1-62414-101-3

Library of Congress Control Number: 2014946095

Cover and book design by Page Street Publishing Co.

Photography by Stephanie Gaudreau

Printed and bound in the U.S.A.

Page Street is proud to be a member of 1% for the Planet. Members donate one percent of their sales to one or more of the over 1,500 environmental and sustainability charities across the globe who participate in this program.

STEPHANIE GAUDREAU
founder of Stupid Easy Paleo

THE PERFORMANCE PALEO COOKBOOK

Recipes for Training Harder, Getting Stronger & Gaining the Competitive Edge

PAGE STREET
PUBLISHING CO.

CONTENTS

FOREWORD

When I heard Steph was writing *The Performance Paleo Cookbook*, I knew she was the perfect person. She's been blogging about nutrition and performance since 2011, and I first got really keyed into her philosophy when she guest-posted on my website. Turns out, Steph's approach is one that's super balanced and sane, and she really cares about helping people excel in sports.

I've been impressed with how Steph walks the talk. She doesn't just write about performance from behind a screen; she's been a lifelong athlete and has adapted a Paleo approach to fueling herself. She's done everything from racing mountain bikes to participating in CrossFit Regionals to competing in Olympic weightlifting. I've watched as she's continued to grow her blog and write a couple books while training several times a week and, most recently, qualifying for the American Open in weightlifting. When you read this book, you can tell Steph gets it.

A dietary foundation rich in animal protein, tons of veggies, some fruit, appropriately-timed dense carbs and a good dose of healthy fat is a solid platform on which to construct a performance-driven athlete. These foods provide the substrate for growth and recovery, are anti-inflammatory and supply a wealth of micronutrition—all critical for folks doing heavy training.

Steph has spelled everything out for you here. Whether you need help with a fueling strategy based on your training time, simple pre- and post-workout snacks, or options for putting together complete meals, she's got you covered. The chapters on protein- and carb-dense recipes, for example, have everything from familiar standbys to novel ingredients that'll get you excited to cook again.

You'll even see some less-traditional options like white potatoes and whey protein pop up in some of the recipes because let's face it, when you're demanding super-human things of your body, you may need to go above and beyond a strict Paleo template to do it. The same way your training should be personalized, making smart additions to an incredibly nutrient-dense, inflammation-fighting Paleo foundation will help you achieve your performance goals.

If you want to do your best athletically, not only do you have to be conscious of food quality and quantity, but it is wise to consume adequate protein and carbohydrates and think about when to eat them. That's what this book does really effectively—Steph's recipes and plan for action will take your performance to the next level.

—Robb Wolf

INTRODUCTION

The pursuit of sport is a fundamental human endeavor that brings us together across countries and cultures. It unifies and connects us. Whether we participate on a team or alone, in formal competitions or against ourselves, sport is an inextricable part of who we are.

When the fire of performance burns within us, training becomes a means to that end. We get up at the break of dawn or head out into the dusky light to train. We lift, run, swim, cycle and jump. We invest in all the right gear our sport requires. But sometimes, despite all these best efforts, we can't seem to fuel our bodies with what they need to really excel.

I wrote this book for anyone who is passionate about performance, whether you train to beat your old personal bests or you put yourself on the competition floor to challenge your limits.

Quality nutrition forms the base of the performance pyramid, and it's even more critical to success than training time, sleep and everything else you do. Eating nutrient-dense, whole foods that provide the energy and substrate for training and recovery is the key to building a solid foundation.

A Paleo template with smart modifications for training is something I personally follow, and it is *the* best way for performance-minded individuals to fortify that foundation. Yes, you *can* get faster and stronger eating this way. Paleo foods are very nutrient-dense. Focusing on quality protein, vegetables, fruit and healthy fats means you get a lot of nutrition bang for your calorie buck. There are a couple of clutch reasons why Paleo is a natural match for athletes.

When training, it's natural to experience acute inflammation as muscles, ligaments and tissues are damaged at the microscopic level. While that sort of inflammatory response is necessary, the type caused by grains, sugar, some dairy and other pro-inflammatory foods is not. By incorporating more anti-inflammatory foods while simultaneously reducing those that cause inflammation, you help your body devote more resources to recovery.

It's necessary to note that eating for performance and eating for aesthetic value are not the same thing. Though maintaining a healthy body composition is important, you must first and foremost eat to support training. Chronically under-fueling or severely restricting one or more of the macronutrients for aesthetic reasons while simultaneously training hard in high-intensity and/or endurance sports leads to eventual declines in performance and, worse, hormonal disarray.

Modifying Paleo for performance means eating enough carbohydrates to support training and recovery and biasing those sources toward whole, nutrient-dense options, such as starchy veggies and fruit. Depending on individual tolerances, you may experiment with starches such as white potatoes, tapioca and even white rice as great sources of post-workout carbohydrates without the issues attached to carb-dense grains and legumes. I recommend you avoid white potatoes and white rice if you're trying to improve your blood sugar management and/or deal with losing significant body fat.

Some starches such as white rice and tapioca are relatively low in nutrient value but high in muscle-refueling glucose, and they're best saved for the post-workout period. In general, you should eat a good whack of carbs after your training session, but it's okay to eat them throughout the day as well.

In terms of protein intake, Paleo performance seekers must get enough protein daily to support muscle repair and recovery along with the myriad other functions this macromolecule serves in our bodies. Animal muscle, organ meats, seafood and eggs are the most nutrient-rich sources of protein. Include them daily at each meal and in pre- and post-workout snacks.

Healthy fats from cold-pressed plant oils like olive and coconut, high-quality animal fats such as clarified butter, ghee, lard and tallow and fatty foods such as nuts, coconut products, egg yolks and olives are excellent sources to use daily. Fats are not only used for energy; they're also integral components of cell membranes, they're hormonal precursors and they assist in the absorption of fat-soluble vitamins.

This cookbook is laid out differently from others you may have read. It starts with chapters for pre- and post-workout snacks, great for smaller portions. Then you'll find recipes for protein- and carb-dense mains and sides, rounded out by chapters devoted to nutrient-dense veggies, sauces and seasonings and healthy treats. Mix and match the recipes from these categories to make meals, or see the chapter on meal combos for 50 different variations. These will help you plan your meals and inspire you to try something new and nutritious.

No matter your sport or your personal goals, the recipes in *The Performance Paleo Cookbook* will help you eat better, train harder, get stronger and gain the competitive edge.

—Stephanie Gaudreau

TEGIES
OUR WORKOUT

...rly riser. The "get up and get it done" folks. Working out in the morning ... rest of the day because you've just come off a fast; from the time ...d no calories. With an early rise and an impending training session, the ... pretty short. Therefore, you've got two options.

...my personal experience and based on people I've worked with, it's not ... generally suboptimal, though purely glycogen-dependent, high-intensity ...

...small amount of food in your belly. I don't recommend a full meal here, ...r waking. Getting up even earlier than normal and missing out on sleep to ...se to make.

The best answer ... amount of protein and fat prior to training.

HERE'S WHAT A SAMPLE DAY MIGHT LOOK LIKE:

FOR FASTED TRAINING BEFORE BREAKFAST
1. Wake
2. No food
3. Train
4. Post-workout refuel
5. Breakfast
6. Lunch
7. Dinner
8. Sleep

(continued)

FOR SEMI-FASTED TRAINING BEFORE BREAKFAST

1. Wake

2. Pre-workout snack

3. Train

4. Post-workout refuel

5. Breakfast

6. Lunch

7. Dinner

8. Sleep

FOR LATE MORNING TRAINING AFTER BREAKFAST

1. Wake

2. Breakfast

3. Train

4. Post-workout refuel

5. Lunch

6. Dinner

7. Sleep

THE NOONER

If you tend to work out around midday, you've had a chance to digest breakfast prior to training. If it's been several hours between breakfast and training, say 5 or 6, it may help to take the edge off your hunger by eating a small pre-workout snack. The disadvantage nooners often have is that they use their lunch break as training time. The post-workout refuel and getting as much nutrition as possible is important.

Those really pressed for time after their workout—getting back to work and on with the day—may roll post-workout refuel in with lunch, essentially eating a larger lunch portion. If that's you, keep fat on the lower side in that meal to aid gastric emptying and faster digestion. Another option is to bring your post-workout refuel to the gym with you and to eat it right after you train. Then eat a normal lunch.

FOR MIDDAY TRAINING (IF YOU DON'T HAVE A LUNCH BREAK)
1. Wake
2. Breakfast
3. Pre-workout snack
4. Train
5. Post-workout refuel + Lunch
6. Dinner
7. Sleep

FOR MIDDAY TRAINING WITH LUNCH BREAK
1. Wake
2. Breakfast
3. Train
4. Post-workout refuel
5. Lunch
6. Dinner
7. Sleep

THE PM TRAINER

The evening crew generally trains after work, and if it's been several hours between lunch and your session, you may want a pre-workout snack to take the edge off any hunger. It's completely individual whether you feel you'll need one. When I ate lunch at noon and trained at 3:30 p.m., I almost never needed to eat again prior to my training session.

If you can't get home and get your post-workout refuel done within 30 minutes of training, bring it to the gym with you. It's easy to get distracted with the commute home and then all the demands of life hitting you once you walk in the door.

If you go to the gym very late in the evening, your post-workout refuel and dinner will likely be combined into one by eating a larger dinner.

FOR EARLY AFTERNOON TRAINING
1. Wake
2. Breakfast
3. Lunch
4. Train
5. Post-workout refuel
6. Dinner
7. Sleep

FOR LATE AFTERNOON/EVENING TRAINING
1. Wake
2. Breakfast
3. Lunch
4. Pre-workout snack
5. Train
6. Post-workout refuel + Dinner
7. Sleep

MEAL COMBO CHART

If you're trying to plan a meal, it helps to have some inspiration for pairing main dishes with sides and accompanying sauces or seasonings. To create a longer-term meal plan, pop some of these combinations in a calendar for the week.

Potato, Leek and Spinach Fritilla (page 66)
Pulled Pork and Sweet Potato Hash (page 94)
Smoky Chipotle Mayo (page 209)

Pizza Burger Bites (page 35)
Zucchini Noodles With Arugula, Bacon and Burst Cherry Tomatoes (page 177)

Tex-Mex Deviled Eggs (page 73)
Smoky Chipotle Mayo (page 209)
Sautéed Spinach

Turkey Veggie Meatloaf (page 36)
Baked Yuca Fries (page 118)
Green Salad

Blueberry Pork Patties (page 58)
Hard-Cooked Eggs
Pulled Pork and Sweet Potato Hash (page 94)

Cocoa Almond Plantain Pancakes (page 54)
Blueberry Pork Patties (page 58)
Sautéed Spinach

Shrimp and Scallop Ceviche (page 77)
Fresh Jicama Sticks
Green Salad

50/50 Meatballs With Blackberry Balsamic Glaze (page 40)
Baked Spaghetti Squash
Swiss Chard Salad With Toasted Walnuts (page 169)

Prosciutto-Wrapped Salmon With Honey Lemon Glaze (page 110)
Baked Cinnamon Carrots (page 121)
Green Salad

Smoked Salmon Egg Bake (page 32)
Roasted Poblano Sauce (page 215)

Musubi Sushi Rolls (page 62)
Strawberry Coconut Kale Salad (page 166)
Sliced Avocado

Apple Fennel Slow Cooker Chicken (page 78)
Duck Fat Roasted Potatoes With Black Garlic (page 131)
Lemon Rosemary Finishing Salt (page 201)

Curried Chicken Salad (page 74)
Hasselback Sweet Potatoes With Compound Herb Ghee (page 139)

Bison and Butternut Skillet (page 65)
Fried Eggs

Breakfast Sausage Scotch Eggs (page 31)
Sautéed Bell Peppers and Onions
Sliced Avocado

Basic Beef Patties (page 39)
Creamy Olive Oil Mayo (page 206)
Baked Yuca Fries (page 118)

Tender Asian-Marinated Flank Steak (page 70)

Chinese Five Spice Kabocha Squash (page 140)

Mocha-Rubbed Slow-Cooker Pot Roast (page 81)

Carrot Parsnip Fritters (page 150)

Green Salad

Spicy Mango Ahi Poke (page 82)

Kicked Up Sriracha (page 216)

Green Salad

Tangy Lemon Dressing (page 211)

Eggplant and Sausage Stacks With Homemade Tomato Sauce (page 93)

Zucchini Noodles With Arugula, Bacon and Burst Cherry Tomatoes (page 177)

Comforting Creamy Broccoli Soup (page 178)

Apple Fennel Slow Cooker Chicken (page 78)

Tender Braised Boneless Beef Short Ribs (page 90)

Creamy Coconut-Braised Sweet Potatoes (page 128)

Sautéed Kale

Larb in Lettuce Wraps (page 85)

Curried Lotus Chips (page 122)

Honey Garlic Lemon Chicken Wings (page 86)

Golden Beet, Fennel and Toasted Hazelnut Salad (page 135)

Roasted Chicken and Asparagus Salad (page 89)

Savory Cauliflower Rice (page 174)

Pulled Pork and Sweet Potato Hash (page 94)

Fried Eggs

Avocado Tomatillo Salsa (page 205)

Badass Bowl (page 97)

Savory Cauliflower Rice (page 174)

Awesomesauce (page 210)

Korean Bibimbap (page 98)

Savory Cauliflower Rice (page 174)

Kicked Up Sriracha (page 216)

Basic Beef Patties (page 39)

Roasted Sweet Potato Salad (page 132)

Lemon Artichoke Chicken (page 101)

Duck Fat Roasted Potatoes With Black Garlic (page 131)

Sautéed Zucchini and Summer Squash

Greek Burger Salad (page 102)

Herbed Olives (page 157)

Mint Basil Brazil Nut Pesto (page 202)

Garlic Lemon Shrimp With Cauliflower Grits (page 105)

Roasted Broccoli

Blackened Fish Soft Tacos With Mango Slaw (page 106)

Blackening Dust (page 198)

Five-Minute Tortillas (page 125)

Roasted Poblano Sauce (page 215)

Panfried Steak With Mushroom Shallot Jus (page 109)

Savory Mushroom Tapioca (page 148)

Roasted Plum Tomatoes With Pancetta (page 165)

Prosciutto-Wrapped Salmon With Honey Lemon Glaze (page 110)

Savory Mushroom Tapioca (page 148)

Sautéed Zucchini

Slow Cooker Lamb Shanks With Tender Root Veggies (page 113)
Green Salad
Tangy Lemon Dressing (page 211)

Spiced Pork Tenderloin With Roasted Plum Sauce (page 114)
Cider-Braised Cabbage, Apple and Onion (page 161)
Baked Cinnamon Carrots (page 121)

Plantain Biscuits (page 126)
Poached Eggs
Mint Basil Brazil Nut Pesto (page 202)

Pulled Pork and Sweet Potato Hash (page 94)
Five-Minute Tortillas (page 125)
Creamy Mango Jalapeño Dressing (page 212)
Tajín Salad (page 170)

Gado Gado With Spicy Satay Sauce (page 173)
Savory Cauliflower Rice (page 174)

Grilled Chicken
Roasted Beets with Orange and Mint (page 143)
Sliced Avocado

Panfried Salmon
Oven-Roasted Sunchokes (page 127)
Sautéed Swiss Chard

Grilled Steak
Twice-Baked Stuffed Sweet Potatoes (page 144)
Sautéed Kale

Mocha-Rubbed Slow-Cooker Pot Roast (page 81)
Creamy Stewed Plantains (page 147)
Braised Collards

Roasted Chicken
Herbed Olives (page 157)
Steamed Kale

Grilled Chicken
Summer Salad With Salt and Pepper Shrimp (page 154)
Tangy Lemon Dressing (page 211)

Crunchy Slaw With Chicken (page 158)
Fresh Watermelon

Pulled Pork and Sweet Potato Hash (page 94)
Strawberry Coconut Kale Salad (page 166)

Baked Salmon
Swiss Chard Salad With Toasted Walnuts (page 169)

Roasted Lamb
Caramelized Brussels Sprouts With Sun-Dried Tomatoes and Pine Nuts (page 162)
Sautéed Spinach

CHAPTER ONE

PRE-WORKOUT

SNACKS

Knowing how to fuel before a workout can be tricky, and it's the part of eating for performance that causes the most confusion. In general, if you've eaten a meal within a few hours of your training session, a separate pre-workout snack isn't needed unless you're really focused on gaining mass or increasing your daily caloric intake.

Given they've properly refueled in the time between training sessions, most people will have topped-off glycogen stores leading up to their workout, so eating more carbohydrates pre-workout isn't necessary. Protein and fat, on the other hand, are effective before a workout. Protein is a source of amino acids needed for muscle protein synthesis and fat provides energy without changing blood sugar levels.

The pre-workout snacks in this chapter are focused on protein and fat, with minimal to no carbohydrates. Depending on your individual tolerance, food eaten before you train is best in the window 15 to 90 minutes before workout.

SUPERCHARGED BUTTER COFFEE

A PRE-WORKOUT PROTEIN AND FAT BOOST

Butter coffee is hot right now—no pun intended. It's coffee made better with the addition of two types of protein, fast-burning medium chain triglycerides (MCT) in coconut oil and healthy saturated fat from grass-fed butter. Couple those with caffeine's ability to enhance your physical performance, and you have a great, rich and creamy option for a morning pre-workout drink that won't leave you feeling weighed down.

MAKES 1 SERVING

1 cup (237 mL) hot brewed coffee

1 tbsp (6 g) protein powder

1 tbsp (7 g) high-quality grass-fed gelatin

1 tsp grass-fed butter or 1 pastured egg yolk

1 tsp coconut oil

1 tsp maca powder, optional

Place all the ingredients in a blender, and process on high until it's nice and creamy.

If you're limiting caffeine, use decaf coffee.

TOTAL RECIPE MACRONUTRIENTS (IN GRAMS PER SERVING)	
PROTEIN	9G
FAT	8G
TOTAL CARB	24G
NET CARB	19G

THE HULK SHAKE

SECRET GREEN HIDES INSIDE THIS MILD-MANNERED SHAKE

If my stomach is rumbling pre-workout, this is one of my go-to shakes. The avocado makes it ultra-creamy without adding the typical coconut or almond milk, and you can't even taste it. Maca is a Peruvian root with adaptogenic benefits. In other words, this nutty shake has superfood status and may help in balancing stress hormones.

MAKES 1 SERVING

1 cup (6 cubes [237 g]) ice

1 cup (237 mL) water

½ avocado (2.5 oz [70 g])

⅓ cup (30 g) protein powder or 2 pastured eggs

1 tbsp (7 g) cocoa powder

1 tsp maca powder

Place all the ingredients in a blender, and process on high until it's nice and creamy.

TOTAL RECIPE MACRONUTRIENTS (IN GRAMS PER SERVING)	
PROTEIN	16G
FAT	12G
TOTAL CARB	20G
NET CARB	8G

MOCHA PROTEIN SHAKE

CHOCOLATY COFFEE GOODNESS PERFECT FOR SIPPING BEFORE YOU TRAIN

Blend up this frosty drink that delivers a punch of protein. It's one of my favorite ways to use up cold coffee. The coconut milk makes it creamy, and adding collagen gives you an extra joint-soothing boost.

MAKES 1 SERVING

1 cup (6 cubes [237 g]) ice

¾ cup (177 mL) water

¼ cup (59 mL) cold coffee

¼ cup (59 mL) full-fat coconut milk

⅓ cup (30 g) protein powder or 2 pastured eggs

1 tbsp (9 g) collagen

1 tbsp (7 g) cocoa powder

Place all the ingredients in a blender, and process on high until it's combined and frothy.

TOTAL RECIPE MACRONUTRIENTS (IN GRAMS PER SERVING)	
PROTEIN	17G
FAT	18G
TOTAL CARB	17G
NET CARB	5G

PUMPKIN PIE SUPERFOOD PUDDING

COMFORTING FLAVORS WITH A NUTRIENT BOOST

Pumpkin pie is one of those quintessential dishes that everybody loves, so I've taken those familiar flavors, ditched the crust and bumped up the nutrient profile by adding protein, MCT oil, maca and chia seeds. The mixture thickens as it sits; the chia naturally absorbs moisture. It can be made a day or two in advance and kept on hand for pre-workout munchies. Pumpkin is especially rich in the antioxidant beta-carotene, which gives it its signature orange color.

MAKES 4 SERVINGS

1 can (15 oz [425 g]) pumpkin puree

½ cup (118 mL) coconut or almond milk

⅓ cup (30 g) protein powder

1 tbsp (15 mL) maple syrup

1 tbsp (15 mL) coconut or MCT oil

1 tbsp (9 g) collagen

2 tsp (10 g) maca powder

1 tsp cinnamon

¼ tsp ground ginger

¼ tsp ground nutmeg

¼ cup (40 g) chia seeds

Place all the ingredients except the chia seeds in a large bowl, and whisk until the mixture is thoroughly combined. Then slowly sprinkle in the chia seeds and whisk the mixture, making sure the seeds don't clump together.

Refrigerate the pudding until the chia seeds have softened a bit and the pudding has thickened, about an hour.

TOTAL RECIPE MACRONUTRIENTS (IN GRAMS PER SERVING)	
PROTEIN	8G
FAT	16G
TOTAL CARB	26G
NET CARB	20G

AVOCADO TOAD IN THE HOLE

These are so simple to make that it's almost criminal. Halve an avocado and scoop out some of the flesh. Then crack an egg into the hole and bake. It reminds me of the toad-in-the-hole eggs on toast we ate as kids, but these just skip the bread. I really love to eat these cold, and they make the perfect snack-size bite loaded with healthy fats.

MAKES 6 SERVINGS

3 avocados (5 oz [140 g each]), halved and pitted

1 tsp garlic powder

½ tsp sea salt

¼ tsp black pepper

6 medium eggs

Preheat the oven to 350°F/177°C and grab a muffin tin.

Scoop about a third of the avocado flesh from each half. You're trying to make just a bit more room for the egg. Sprinkle the avocado with garlic powder, salt and pepper.

Arrange each avocado half so it's sitting on top of the holes of the muffin tin. Gently crack an egg into each half.

Bake these for 12 to 15 minutes or until the white is set. I recommend eating them cold.

TOTAL RECIPE MACRONUTRIENTS (IN GRAMS PER SERVING)	
PROTEIN	7G
FAT	13G
TOTAL CARB	5G
NET CARB	4G

SWEET AND SPICY OVEN-BAKED JERKY

A CLASSIC FAVORITE, MADE RIGHT IN YOUR OVEN

Jerky is by far one of my favorite snacks, but finding a clean source without ordering online is really hard. By slicing the steak very thinly, marinating it and drying it for a couple of hours in the oven, you'll end up with your own protein-packed snack. The combination of the sweet pineapple juice with the salty coconut aminos and the spice from the red pepper flakes will keep you coming back for more. Plus, pineapple is high in bromelain, a combination of enzymes noted for its anti-inflammatory properties.

MAKES 16 SERVINGS

1 ½ lb (680 g) London broil or other lean steak

2 cups (473 mL) pineapple juice

¼ cup (59 mL) coconut aminos

1 tbsp (15 g) sea salt

2 tsp (6 g) red pepper flakes

To prep the steak, freeze it most of the way through to make it easier to slice. Using a very sharp knife, slice the steak against the grain and on the bias to make wide strips. You need to slice the steak very thinly, about ¹⁄₁₆ inch/1.5 millimeters.

To make the marinade, in a medium bowl or large plastic zip-top bag, combine the pineapple juice, coconut aminos, salt and red pepper flakes. Stir until the salt dissolves, then add the steak. Marinate the steak 12 to 24 hours for best results.

Next, bake the jerky. Preheat the oven to 200°F/93°C and line two baking sheets with foil. You'll also need two metal baking racks. Lay one on top each sheet. Drain and discard the marinade. Arrange the steak slices in a single layer, making sure the pieces don't overlap. Bake about 2 hours or until the steak is very dry. You want to make sure there's no moisture left in the jerky. Cool and store for up to a week in the refrigerator, tightly covered.

You can also use a dehydrator to make the jerky. Follow the manufacturer's instructions.

TOTAL RECIPE MACRONUTRIENTS (IN GRAMS PER SERVING)

PROTEIN	12G
FAT	3G
TOTAL CARB	5G
NET CARB	5G

BREAKFAST SAUSAGE SCOTCH EGGS

HARD-COOKED EGGS SHROUDED IN A MEATY COAT

In most of the world, Scotch eggs are sold as pub food and deep-fried with a crunchy coating. Hardly a healthy dish. With a few minor alterations, these nuggets are a great pre-workout snack. If you can't find pork rinds—also known as Chicharrón—with just pork and salt as the ingredients, feel free to leave them out. The Scotch eggs are still flavorful without them.

MAKES 6 SERVINGS

6 medium eggs

1 lb (454 g) ground pork

¾ tsp cinnamon

¾ tsp ground ginger

¾ tsp allspice

½ tsp black pepper

⅛ tsp ground nutmeg

⅛ tsp ground cloves

½ tbsp (8 g) sea salt

1 tbsp (15 mL) raw honey, optional

2 cups (36 g) pork rinds, crushed, optional

Start by hard-cooking the eggs. My tried-and-true method is to steam them because the shells slip right off. Place a medium pot on the stovetop, and fit it with a steamer basket. Fill the bottom of the pot with 1 inch/2.5 centimeters of water, then put the lid on and bring the water to a boil. Once the water boils, remove the eggs from the refrigerator and place them in the steamer basket. Be careful: Steam can burn you! Replace the lid and steam the eggs for 10 minutes. Meanwhile, fill a medium bowl with water and several ice cubes. When your timer goes off, turn off the heat and move the eggs to the ice water. Cool completely, then peel them.

Preheat the oven to 350°F/177°C and line a baking sheet with foil or parchment paper.

In a large bowl, combine the ground pork, spices, salt and honey. Mix until combined but only for about 15 seconds or so. Don't overdo it; that'll make the meat tough.

Now assemble the Scotch eggs. For each egg: Take ⅓ cup/76 grams of the seasoned ground pork and turn the meat out into your hand. Flatten the pork into a wide circle like you're making a burger. Put the peeled egg in the center. Carefully fold the meat circle upward, smoothing it as you go. Roll the Scotch egg in the crushed pork rinds.

Place the Scotch eggs on the sheet, and bake for 15 to 20 minutes or until the meat is fully cooked through.

Substitute ground beef for the pork.

TOTAL RECIPE MACRONUTRIENTS (IN GRAMS PER SERVING)	
PROTEIN	23G
FAT	23G
TOTAL CARB	4G
NET CARB	4G

SMOKED SALMON EGG BAKE

PORTABLE PRE-WORKOUT PROTEIN WITH A SMOKED SALMON TWIST

With their protein and healthy fat profile, eggs make a fantastic pre-workout food. They're rich in essential nutrients like vitamin D, choline and folate and are a relatively inexpensive way to incorporate more protein into your diet. In this recipe, I bumped up the veggie content with the zucchini and green onions. Cut into squares, and take them with you on the go!

MAKES 6 SERVINGS

1 tsp + 1 tbsp (15 mL) coconut oil

1 lb (454 g) zucchini, shredded

3 green onions (2 oz [57 g]), white and light green parts, thinly sliced

1 tsp sea salt

½ tsp black pepper

8 large eggs, beaten

1 tsp dried dill

4 oz (113 g) smoked salmon, chopped

Preheat the oven to 350°F/177°C and grease an 8-inch x 8-inch/20-centimeter x 20-centimeter baking dish with 1 teaspoon coconut oil.

Now sweat the zucchini and green onions. Heat a large skillet over medium heat, then add 1 tablespoon/15 milliliters coconut oil. Add the zucchini, green onions, salt and pepper. Cook and stir until the veggies are wilted and lightly browned. You want most of the moisture to cook off, about 6 to 8 minutes. Let the mixture cool.

Meanwhile, in a large bowl, beat the eggs together with the dill, then mix in the smoked salmon. When the zucchini and green onions are cool, add them to the eggs and stir until everything is well combined. Pour the mixture into the baking dish. Bake for 30 to 35 minutes or until the center is set and not liquid.

TOTAL RECIPE MACRONUTRIENTS (IN GRAMS PER SERVING)	
PROTEIN	13G
FAT	11G
TOTAL CARB	3G
NET CARB	2G

PIZZA BURGER BITES

Inspired by my love of pizza, I wanted these protein-dense meatballs to pack a punch of flavor reminiscent of a traditional combination pie. The sausage adds taste, and the beef keeps it from being too heavy. You can get really creative and add in your favorite "toppings" to customize the flavor.

MAKES 4 SERVINGS

½ lb (227 g) ground beef

½ lb (227 g) sausage

¼ cup (32 g) chopped black olives

¼ cup (45 g) roasted red peppers, chopped

2 tsp (4 g) dried oregano

½ tsp sea salt

¼ tsp black pepper

1 tbsp (15 mL) coconut oil

2 tbsp (5 g) chopped fresh parsley, garnish

Tomato sauce for dipping, optional

Preheat the oven to 350°F/177°C, and line a large baking sheet with foil or parchment paper.

In a large bowl, mix all the ingredients together until blended, but don't overwork the meat—that'll make for tough meatballs. At this point, take a small pinch of the meat, fry it in the skillet and taste to check the seasoning level. If it needs more salt and pepper, add it now. Form the mixture into meatballs, about 1 tablespoon/15 grams meat for each. Put these on a plate.

Heat a large skillet over medium-high heat and add 1 tablespoon/15 milliliters coconut oil. Add one layer of meatballs to the skillet. Don't overcrowd the meatballs because they won't brown evenly. Fry for about 2 minutes per side—I usually do 4 "sides"—so a nice brown crust forms, then place them on the baking sheet. Repeat with the rest of the meatballs.

Bake the meatballs for about 15 minutes or until they're cooked through completely. Sprinkle with fresh chopped parsley. Serve with a side of prepared tomato sauce for dipping.

If you can't find sausage without a bunch of artificial ingredients, use ½ pound/227 grams fresh ground pork instead.

TOTAL RECIPE MACRONUTRIENTS (IN GRAMS PER SERVING)

PROTEIN	16G
FAT	44G
TOTAL CARB	2G
NET CARB	1G

TURKEY VEGGIE MEATLOAF

SAVORY MEATLOAF WITH HIDDEN VEGGIES

As a kid, I did everything I could to avoid meatloaf because it was dense and bland. I went on a mission to bring you a lighter version with great taste and more nutrient value than just plain meat. If you're looking for a little nosh that's loaded with lean protein, this is the one for you. Make a pan on your weekly cook-up day and enjoy grab-and-go pre-workout protein at your fingertips.

MAKES 8 SERVINGS

1 tsp + 1 tbsp (15 mL) coconut oil

1 small zucchini (6 oz [170 g]), grated

1 large carrot (3 oz [85 g]), grated

1 large stalk celery (2 oz [57 g]), finely chopped

½ medium onion (5 oz [142 g]), finely chopped

2 cloves garlic, finely chopped

1 tsp ground sage

½ tsp sea salt

¼ tsp black pepper

1 ¼ lb (567 g) ground turkey

2 tsp (10 mL) Dijon mustard

½ tsp fish sauce

Preheat the oven to 375°F/191°C, and grease an 8-inch x 8-inch/20-centimeter x 20-centimeter baking dish with 1 teaspoon of coconut oil.

Heat a large skillet over medium-high heat, then add the rest of the coconut oil. Cook and stir the zucchini, carrot, celery, onion, garlic, sage, salt and pepper until the veggies soften, about 5 to 7 minutes. Allow this to cool before the next step.

Add the ground turkey, Dijon mustard and fish sauce to a large bowl. Then pour the cooked veggies in. Mix all the ingredients until they're combined but not overworked. At this point, take a small pinch of the meat, fry it in the skillet and taste to check the seasoning level. If it needs more salt and pepper, add it now. Gently press the mixture into the baking dish, and bake for about 20 minutes or until completely cooked through.

You can't taste the fish sauce, but it adds a layer of savory "umami" flavor.

TOTAL RECIPE MACRONUTRIENTS (IN GRAMS PER SERVING)	
PROTEIN	13G
FAT	8G
TOTAL CARB	4G
NET CARB	3G

BASIC BEEF PATTIES

THE DO-IT-ALL BASE FOR ALL YOUR BURGER CREATIONS

Every cookbook needs a recipe for the perfect burger, and this is my contribution. I've pulled inspiration from two of my Paleo heroes: Melissa Joulwan of The Clothes Make the Girl and Michelle Tam of Nom Nom Paleo. Ever since Mel came out with *Well Fed 2,* I've been using her method for tenderizing burgers because it's foolproof. The meat comes out tender with a really nice crust. I've also taken a page from Michelle's umami files, and you'll see dried, powdered shiitake mushrooms show up as a flavor enhancer throughout the book.

MAKES 4 SERVINGS

1 ½ lb (680 g) ground beef

1 tbsp (15 mL) water

¼ tsp cream of tartar

⅛ tsp baking soda

2 tbsp (6 g) ground, dried shiitake mushrooms

1 tsp onion powder

¾ tsp sea salt

½ tsp black pepper

1 tbsp (15 mL) coconut oil

Place the ground beef in a large bowl. In a small bowl, mix the water, cream of tartar and baking soda. Pour this onto the ground beef, and let it sit for 5 minutes. Then add the rest of the seasonings. At this point, take a small pinch of the meat, fry it in the skillet and taste to check the seasoning level. If it needs more salt and pepper, add it now. Mix the beef and seasonings with your hands until combined but not overworked. Shape the meat into 8 patties. A dimple pressed into the top of the burger will keep it flat during cooking.

Heat a large skillet on medium-high and add the coconut oil. Fry the burgers for about 4 minutes on each side.

Top with your choice of veggies and condiments. A little sauerkraut on top is always a favorite!

TOTAL RECIPE MACRONUTRIENTS (IN GRAMS PER SERVING)	
PROTEIN	29G
FAT	49G
TOTAL CARB	2G
NET CARB	2G

50/50 MEATBALLS WITH BLACKBERRY BALSAMIC GLAZE

BEEF AND BACON GET FRIENDLY IN THESE MEATBALLS

Where I live, there's a famous restaurant that makes burger patties with half bacon, half beef. This recipe's a play on that succulent combination, and the tangy blackberry glaze is a simple way to add a ton of flavor. Serve these with extra glaze on the side for dipping!

MAKES 4 SERVINGS

1 lb (454 g) very lean ground beef

1 tbsp (15 mL) water

¼ tsp cream of tartar

⅛ tsp baking soda

¼ lb (113 g) bacon, finely chopped

½ tsp sea salt

¾ tsp black pepper

1 tbsp (9 g) dried onion flakes

1 tbsp (3 g) chopped fresh rosemary

1 tsp fresh thyme

1 tbsp (15 mL) coconut oil

6 oz (170 g) blackberries

¼ cup (59 mL) balsamic vinegar

Preheat the oven to 350°F/177°C and line a baking sheet with foil or parchment paper.

To make the meatballs, place the ground beef in a large bowl. In a small bowl, mix the water, cream of tartar and baking soda. Pour this onto the ground beef, and let sit for 5 minutes. Meanwhile, roughly chop the bacon, and add it to a food processor. Pulse to break it down so that it is finely chopped. Add the bacon, salt, pepper, onion flakes, rosemary and thyme to the ground beef. Mix with your hands until combined but not overworked. At this point, take a small pinch of the meat, fry it in the skillet and taste to check the seasoning level. If it needs more salt and pepper, add it now. Shape the meat into 12 meatballs.

Heat a large skillet over medium-high heat, and add 1 tablespoon/15 milliliters coconut oil. Heat until the oil is shimmering, then add one layer of meatballs to the skillet. Don't overcrowd the meatballs or they won't brown evenly. Fry for about 2 minutes per side—I usually do 4 "sides"—so a nice brown crust forms, then place on the baking sheet. Repeat with the rest of the meatballs. Place them on the baking sheet, and bake for about 15 to 20 minutes or until they're cooked through completely.

While the meatballs are baking, make the glaze. In a small pot, combine the blackberries with the balsamic vinegar. Mash the berries with the back of a spoon to release the juice while you bring it to a boil, then reduce to a simmer. Simmer on low for 10 to 15 minutes or until the liquid is reduced by about half. Strain the glaze through a fine mesh strainer to remove the seeds. Spoon the glaze over the cooked meatballs when they come out of the oven, and save any extra glaze for dipping.

You can omit the bacon, but be sure to choose a ground beef with higher fat content to keep these moist.

TOTAL RECIPE MACRONUTRIENTS (IN GRAMS PER SERVING)	
PROTEIN	29G
FAT	41G
TOTAL CARB	8G
NET CARB	5G

CHAPTER TWO

POST-WORKOUT

REFUEL

Protein and carbs. When it comes to post-workout refueling, remember that combination. Eating after a workout is often considered an optional bonus meal, but for people training hard, it's a necessity and has a twofold purpose. First, protein is a source of amino acids, which help rebuild muscle so you recover from your training efforts. Second, carbohydrates replenish your stores of glycogen, a fuel source for high-intensity and shorter endurance training. Right after a workout, your body is more sensitive to insulin so post-training carbs are shuttled back into your cells. When it comes to carbohydrates, though, not all are created equal.

As much as possible, go for starchy carbohydrates—like nutrient-dense root vegetables and potatoes—and potentially other safe starches such as tapioca and white rice. These starches break down into glucose which refills muscle glycogen, getting you ready for the next training session. Fruit, on the other hand, contains fructose, a type of sugar that preferentially replenishes glycogen in the liver instead of muscles. While fruit is better than nothing, if you bias your choices toward starchy carbohydrates most of the time, you'll refuel your muscle most efficiently.

The post-workout refuel recipes in this chapter are focused on protein and carbs, with minimal to no fat. Eating a large amount of fat slows stomach emptying, making the digestion of your post-workout take longer when time is absolutely of the essence. In general, eat your post-workout meal as soon after training as you can; shoot for 15 to 30 minutes after workout as the optimal range. Keep in mind, the sooner your next training session comes around, the more crucial it is to refuel right away.

GREEN IMMUNITY BOOST VEGGIE JUICE

Good gut integrity is one of the keys to staying healthy. This green drink makes an almost daily appearance on my menu, and I serve it up blended and unstrained. I like the pulp, and getting the fiber along with the veggies and fruit is important. If you prefer a smoother consistency, you can run this through a juicer or strain it after blending. Kombucha has probiotics which help maintain a healthy gut flora. The ginger, turmeric and garlic are renowned for their anti-inflammatory and antibacterial properties. While I'm a big proponent of chewing your food, for busy folks, one green juice a day helps supplement vitamins and minerals you might otherwise miss if you skipped out. This is best consumed with a source of protein for post-workout, such as the Basic Beef Patties (page 39).

MAKES 2 SERVINGS

1 ½ cups (355 mL) water

½ cup (118 mL) kombucha

2 cups (76 g) packed spinach

1 carrot, top removed and chopped

½ medium red apple, cored and chopped

1" (2.5 cm) piece ginger, peeled and sliced into thin coins

1" (2.5 cm) piece turmeric, peeled

½ clove garlic

Place all the ingredients in a powerful blender, and whiz until everything is smooth, about 15 seconds. Serve over ice.

Add kale instead of spinach for a different micronutrient profile.

TOTAL RECIPE MACRONUTRIENTS (IN GRAMS PER SERVING)	
PROTEIN	2G
FAT	1G
TOTAL CARB	16G
NET CARB	12G

COCONUT WATER ELECTROLYTE DRINK

Coconut water is the darling of Paleo hydration drinks because it's a natural source of electrolytes, but it's got a flaw. It's relatively poor in sodium, an essential electrolyte needed for proper muscle and nerve function. To improve it, I've added sea salt for sodium and pineapple juice for a decent source of fruit-based glucose.

MAKES 4 SERVINGS

2 cups (473 mL) unsweetened coconut water

1 cup (237 mL) unsweetened pineapple juice

¼ tsp sea salt

Mix all the ingredients in a glass jar, and store it in the refrigerator for up to 3 days.

TOTAL RECIPE MACRONUTRIENTS (IN GRAMS PER SERVING)

PROTEIN	1G
FAT	TRACE
TOTAL CARB	13G
NET CARB	13G

PINEAPPLE ORANGE POPSICLES

ELECTROLYTE REPLACING POPSICLES, PERFECT FOR HOT TRAINING DAYS

Just finsihed training on a summer day? These popsicles are a fun way to rehydrate smart. Coconut water gets a better electrolyte profile with the addition of sea salt, and the pineapple juice has more glucose content than most fruit.

MAKES 8 TO 10 SERVINGS

Zest of 1 orange

1 large orange, skin and pith removed

2 cups (473 mL) unsweetened pineapple juice

2 cups (473 mL) unsweetened coconut water

¼ tsp sea salt

Combine all the ingredients in a high-powered blender and process until the mixture is smooth, about 15 seconds. Pour into popsicle molds and freeze until solid, at least 2 or 3 hours.

TOTAL RECIPE MACRONUTRIENTS (IN GRAMS PER SERVING)

PROTEIN	1G
FAT	TRACE
TOTAL CARB	10G
NET CARB	10G

CHERRY VANILLA SHAKE

Shakes are popular for pre- and post-workout nutrition because they're easy to consume. One thing you'll want to avoid is adding coconut milk or nut milk as the entire liquid base for your shakes because each adds a lot of fat. From a digestive standpoint, a large amount of fat slows gastric emptying, delaying digestion and replenishment of nutrients to the muscles. In general, if your next training session is hours and not days away, keep your post-workout refuel low in fat.

MAKES 1 SERVING

1 cup (237 mL) water

½ cup (3 cubes [118 g]) ice

½ cup (120 g) frozen cherries

⅓ cup (30 g) vanilla protein powder or 2 pastured eggs

Place all the ingredients in a blender, and process on high until it's nice and creamy, about 30 seconds.

You can use chocolate protein powder instead of vanilla.

TOTAL RECIPE MACRONUTRIENTS (IN GRAMS PER SERVING)	
PROTEIN	13G
FAT	10G
TOTAL CARB	9G
NET CARB	9G

TROPICAL TARO SHAKE

CREAMY, WITH A TASTE OF THE TROPICS

It was on a vacation to Kauai when I first ran across the idea of a taro shake. Taro is a carb-dense root used in a lot of Polynesian/Hawaiian cooking. When blended into a frozen post-workout drink, the taro puree gives it a creamy texture without the addition of fat, which slows digestion. Make up a large batch of taro puree, and then freeze it into cubes for a convenient carb addition to any shake. Taro, available at Asian markets, is relatively inexpensive.

MAKES 1 SERVING

¼ cup frozen Taro Puree, about 2 cubes (page 149)

½ cup (121 g) frozen mango

½ cup (83 g) frozen pineapple

½ cup (118 mL) water

⅓ cup (30 g) protein powder or 2 pastured eggs

Place all the ingredients in a blender and process on high until it's nice and creamy, about 30 seconds.

Try adding other frozen fruit such as strawberries or bananas.

TOTAL RECIPE MACRONUTRIENTS (IN GRAMS PER SERVING)	
PROTEIN	15G
FAT	4G
TOTAL CARB	67G
NET CARB	49G

BANANA COCOA PROTEIN PACKS

Single-use post-workout fuel packs are starting to pop up from different manufacturers as the need for quick and portable nutrition packs is being realized. For some, the cost is worth it, but for others, it's prohibitive. If you're of the do-it-yourself mind-set, you can easily whip up your own really tasty carb and protein replacement, freeze it ahead of time and defrost it as needed.

MAKES 5 SERVINGS

4 ripe bananas (1 ½ lb [680 g]), peeled and chopped

⅓ cup (30 g) protein powder

¼ cup (28 g) cocoa powder

2 tbsp (10 mL) coconut or almond milk

Place all the ingredients in a blender or food processor, and process until the mixture is smooth, about 15 seconds.

Freeze this in small plastic zip-top bags for portable post-workout carbs.

TOTAL RECIPE MACRONUTRIENTS (IN GRAMS PER SERVING)	
PROTEIN	9G
FAT	4G
TOTAL CARB	30G
NET CARB	21G

APRICOT CARROT GINGER PUREE

A DELICIOUS FRUIT-BASED POST-WORKOUT CARB SOURCE

Fruit isn't my number-one pick for post-workout carbs simply because it's not as rich in glucose as starchy sources. Sometimes, though, it's nice to switch it up and add variety to your routine. This puree is inspired by the very popular baby food packets with different fruit and veggie combinations, and making it yourself saves money. I've added ginger and turmeric to bump up the anti-inflammatory power! Combine this with a protein such as the Basic Beef Patties (page 39) for a complete post-workout meal.

MAKES 8 SERVINGS

1 ½ lb (680 g) apricots, halved and pitted

1 lb (454 g) carrots, tops removed and chopped

¾ lb (340 g) pears, cored and chopped

1" (2.5 cm) piece ginger, peeled and sliced into thin coins

½ cup (118 mL) water

2 tbsp (30 mL) lemon juice

1 tsp cinnamon

½ tsp ground turmeric

⅛ tsp sea salt

Combine all the ingredients in a large pot with a lid. Bring to a boil then reduce to a simmer for about 25 minutes or until the fruit has softened. Remove the lid, and simmer for about 5 more minutes or until the mixture has thickened. Let the mixture cool, then puree in a high-powered blender or food processor until smooth, about 15 seconds.

Freeze this in plastic zip-top bags for portable post-workout carbs.

TOTAL RECIPE MACRONUTRIENTS (IN GRAMS PER SERVING)	
PROTEIN	2G
FAT	1G
TOTAL CARB	21G
NET CARB	17G

COCOA ALMOND PLANTAIN PANCAKES

PLANTAINS ARE THE NEW SWEET POTATO

If you're suffering from sweet potato burnout, try swapping plantains into your routine. They can be cooked and eaten green (starchier) or ripe (sweeter), and they are an excellent source of post-workout carbohydrates and potassium. They're great in both savory and sweet applications, and here they take the place of fructose-rich bananas in these simple pancakes.

MAKES 2 SERVINGS

1 ½ lb (680 g) ripe yellow plantains, peeled and roughly chopped

2 large eggs

3 tbsp (18 g) protein powder

2 tbsp (12 g) cocoa powder

1 tbsp (7 g) arrowroot flour

1 tbsp (16 g) almond butter

½ tsp vanilla extract

¼ tsp almond extract, optional

Place all the ingredients in a high-powered blender or food processor, and blend until the batter is smooth.

Heat a cast iron skillet over medium-low heat, then reduce the heat to low for the remainder of the cooking. Drop about 2 tablespoons/30 milliliters of the batter into the skillet to make each pancake. So you don't crowd the pancakes, you'll have to do this in more than one batch. Cook for about 2 minutes, then flip and cook for another minute. Remove and place on a cooling rack.

TOTAL RECIPE MACRONUTRIENTS (IN GRAMS PER SERVING)

PROTEIN	19G
FAT	13G
TOTAL CARB	40G
NET CARB	19G

CHERRY CASHEW PROTEIN BARS

This recipe is definitely for the open-minded because I've taken the idea of a basic fruit and nut bar and added cricket flour for protein. Why crickets? They're a really sustainable, convenient source of protein that tastes good, like toasted nuts. Nutritionally speaking, cricket flour is very high in iron, calcium and B vitamins—higher than equal measures of beef.

MAKES 8 SERVINGS

¾ cup (100 g) chopped unroasted cashews

¼ cup (32 g) cashew flour

½ cup (20 g) cricket flour

¼ tsp sea salt

6 large (120 g) Medjool dates, pitted

½ cup (90 g) dried blueberries

¾ cup (100 g) dried cherries

1 tsp vanilla extract

Coconut oil

Line an 8-inch x 8-inch/20-centimeter x 20-centimeter glass dish with plastic wrap or waxed paper and set aside.

Place the chopped cashews, cashew flour, cricket flour and sea salt in a food processor and pulse until they form coarse crumbs. Some pieces of the nuts may be larger and some smaller; that's okay. Pour out into a medium bowl.

Now add the dates, blueberries, cherries and vanilla extract to the food processor, and process this until it comes together and forms a sticky ball. Add this to the chopped nut mixture. Add a few drops of coconut oil to your hands to keep everything from sticking. Work the fruit and nuts together with your hands until everything is combined. You'll have to work at it a bit! Place it into the glass dish, and press it down until it's one even layer. Freeze this for 30 minutes, then turn it out onto a cutting board and slice into bars with a sharp knife. Wrap them in plastic for storage.

I like to store these in the freezer for up to a month.

TOTAL RECIPE MACRONUTRIENTS (IN GRAMS PER SERVING)	
PROTEIN	16G
FAT	7G
TOTAL CARB	45G
NET CARB	41G

BLUEBERRY PORK PATTIES

PORK GETS AN UNEXPECTEDLY DELICIOUS BERRY BOOST

These patties were inspired by a flavor of bulk sausage sold at one of my local markets, but premade varieties often contain preservatives or fillers. I was determined to make my own. Blueberries lend a bit of sweetness that's perfect for breakfast sausage and pair well with the tarragon and fennel. Bonus: Blueberries are rich in antioxidants, which help ward off cellular damage.

MAKES 4 SERVINGS

1 lb (454 g) lean ground pork

½ cup (75 g) blueberries, chopped

½ tbsp (2 g) dried tarragon

½ tsp fennel seeds

½ tsp sea salt

¼ tsp black pepper

1 tbsp (15 mL) coconut oil

In a large bowl, combine the pork, blueberries, tarragon, fennel, salt and pepper. Mix gently with your hands until everything is well combined but not overworked. At this point, take a small pinch of the meat and fry it in the skillet to check the seasoning level. If it needs more salt and pepper, add it now. Form the meat into 8 small patties.

Heat a large skillet over medium-high heat, and melt the coconut oil. Fry the patties for 4 minutes on each side or until completely cooked through.

If you can't find berries or they're not in season, frozen blueberries will work. Just chop roughly while still frozen, and toss them in.

TOTAL RECIPE MACRONUTRIENTS (IN GRAMS PER SERVING)	
PROTEIN	19G
FAT	28G
TOTAL CARB	3G
NET CARB	2G

SALMON CAKES WITH CAPERS AND DILL

OMEGA-3-RICH SALMON IS THE STAR OF THESE GLUTEN-FREE CAKES

This is probably the perfect post-workout nosh. It's got wild salmon, which is rich in anti-inflammatory Omega-3 fatty acids, and potatoes, which are an excellent source of carbohydrates. White potatoes sometimes get a bad rap, but as long as you tolerate nightshades and you aren't dealing with blood sugar issues, they're great for replenishing glycogen after you train.

MAKES 9 CAKES

8 oz (227 g) red-skinned potatoes

1 tsp coconut oil

2 (6 oz [170 g]) cans wild salmon, drained

1 large egg, beaten

2 tbsp (24 g) capers, chopped

2 tsp (10 mL) brown mustard

1 tbsp (14 g) dried dill

1 tsp hot sauce

¼ tsp black pepper

Preheat the oven to 400°F/204°C and line a baking sheet with foil or parchment paper. Roast the red potatoes on the sheet for about 40 minutes or until they're tender when poked with a fork. Let them cool, then trim the skins off and mash gently in a large bowl with a fork. Place a fresh piece of parchment paper—not foil, they'll stick—on the baking sheet and grease the paper with the coconut oil. I use my fingers to spread the oil around.

Add the rest of the ingredients to the potatoes and stir well to combine. Pack the mixture into a ¼-cup/59-milliliter measuring cup and turn it out onto the parchment paper. Repeat until you've used up all of the mixture.

Bake the salmon cakes at 400°F/204°C for 10 minutes, then flip them over with a spatula. Bake for another 5 minutes and cool on a wire rack.

For a change of pace, substitute sweet potatoes for white.

TOTAL RECIPE MACRONUTRIENTS (IN GRAMS PER SERVING)

PROTEIN	9G
FAT	2G
TOTAL CARB	5G
NET CARB	5G

MUSUBI SUSHI ROLLS

ALL THE FLAVOR OF THIS TRADITIONAL HAWAIIAN TREAT WITHOUT THE SOY AND GLUTEN

A few years back, I tried musubi for the first time. It's basically a slice of Spam that's been coated with a soy sauce and sugar glaze, then sandwiched between slabs of white rice and wrapped in nori (seaweed wrappers). It's really delicious, but I wanted to make a version without the soy and processed meat, so this idea was born. White rice is a great post-workout carbohydrate source, and the nori is rich in iodine, an essential nutrient needed for healthy thyroid function.

MAKES 4 SERVINGS

1 cup (180 g) uncooked sushi rice

2 cups (473 mL) chicken broth

1 oz (28 g) dates, about 2 large Medjool dates, pitted

¼ cup (59 mL) boiling water

¼ cup (59 mL) coconut aminos

½ lb (227 g) cooked pulled pork

5 sheets untoasted nori (seaweed wrappers)

2 ½ tsp (7 g) furikake, gomasio or toasted sesame seeds

¼ cup (59 mL) water

Cook the sushi rice with the chicken broth according to the package time directions. Set aside.

Place the dates in a heat-resistant container. Pour the boiling water over the top and let the dates soften for about 10 minutes. Then pour the dates, water and coconut aminos into a food processor or blender. Process until smooth, then pour the mixture into a small pot. Bring the mixture to a boil, then reduce to a simmer for about 5 minutes or until it thickens. Turn off the heat and stir in the cooked pulled pork until it's evenly coated. Set aside.

Now start constructing each roll. Place the shiny side of the nori down on a cutting board or flat surface. Place a small scoop of rice onto the nori and smooth it into an even layer across the bottom third of the sheet, from edge to edge. On top of that, add a small amount of pulled pork, and smooth that into an even layer. Sprinkle with ½ teaspoon furikake.

Time to roll the sushi up. Place ¼ cup/59 milliliters water in a small bowl. Starting at the edge closest to you, tightly roll the nori, rice and pork up toward the top. When you're within 1 inch/2.5 centimeters of the top, dip your finger in the water and moisten the top edge of the nori. This will help it stick so it doesn't come apart. Then finish rolling it up. Put the sushi aside and repeat the process until you've used up all the nori, rice, pork and furikake.

After 10 minutes, use a very sharp knife to slice the roll into small pieces, about 6 per roll.

Sub cauliflower rice for white rice, and serve it in a bowl, deconstructed-style, with the the pork and nori on top.

TOTAL RECIPE MACRONUTRIENTS (IN GRAMS PER SERVING)	
PROTEIN	17G
FAT	11G
TOTAL CARB	47G
NET CARB	45G

BISON AND BUTTERNUT SKILLET

This is hands-down one of the easiest and most comforting dishes I eat on a regular basis, and it's definitely filling. Consider this recipe like a template you can customize for your tastes and what you have on hand in the fridge. Feel free to sub out the bison for any other protein of choice, the squash for sweet potato and the Swiss chard for spinach or kale, for example. The world is really your oyster on this one!

MAKES 4 SERVINGS

1 tbsp (15 mL) coconut oil

1 lb (454 g) ground bison

½ tsp sea salt

¼ tsp black pepper

½ lb (227 g) diced roasted butternut squash

1 medium bunch Swiss chard (9 oz [255 g]), stems removed and leaves chopped

¼ cup (59 mL) full-fat coconut milk

¼ tsp cinnamon

¼ tsp dried thyme

Heat a large skillet over medium-high heat, then add 1 tablespoon/15 milliliters coconut oil. Crumble the ground bison into the skillet, and season it with salt and pepper. Use a wooden spoon to break up the meat, stirring occasionally until the meat is browned and cooked through, about 5 to 7 minutes. Lower the heat to medium-low and add the squash, Swiss chard, coconut milk, cinnamon and thyme. Stir until everything's well combined and warmed through, about 3 to 5 minutes.

Make a double batch of this on your weekly cook-up day!

TOTAL RECIPE MACRONUTRIENTS (IN GRAMS PER SERVING)	
PROTEIN	25G
FAT	9G
TOTAL CARB	7G
NET CARB	6G

POTATO, LEEK AND SPINACH FRITILLA

WHAT HAPPENS WHEN AN ITALIAN FRITTATA MEETS A SPANISH TORTILLA

In my mind, eggs are a perfect post-workout food, and the addition of potatoes to this dish makes it better. This makes a large batch that's great to take along with you for after training, and the fact that it's portable and finger-food friendly is even better. You can always substitute sweet potatoes for white if you're avoiding nightshades.

MAKES 6 SERVINGS

1 large leek (8 oz [227 g]), white and light green parts, chopped

⅛ tsp + ½ tsp sea salt

1 tbsp (15 g) + 1 tbsp (15 g) + 1 tsp ghee

6 cups (12 oz [340 g]) spinach, tough stems removed

1 lb (454 g) russet potatoes, peeled and sliced into ¼" (6 mm) pieces

10 large eggs, beaten

¼ tsp black pepper

¼ tsp cayenne pepper

Preheat the oven to 350°F/177°C.

Start by sweating down the leeks. In a large cast-iron skillet over medium-high heat, cook and stir the leeks, ⅛ teaspoon salt and 1 tablespoon/15 grams ghee until the leeks are softened and lightly browned, about 5 minutes. Add the spinach to the same skillet and stir until the spinach wilts but doesn't get soggy, about 2 minutes. Set the mixture aside in a medium bowl to cool.

In the same skillet over medium heat, melt another tablespoon/15 grams ghee, and then add the sliced potatoes and ½ teaspoon salt. Cook and stir the potatoes until they begin to brown, about 5 minutes. Remove the potatoes from the skillet and set them aside to cool.

In a medium bowl, beat the eggs with ½ teaspoon salt and the black and cayenne peppers.

Now build the fritilla in the same cast-iron skillet. Melt 1 teaspoon ghee into the pan, and rub it around to add insurance against sticking. Then layer the potatoes in the bottom of the skillet, and put the leek/spinach mixture on top. Pour the beaten egg mixture into the pan, and use a spatula to move the potatoes, leeks and spinach around just a bit, so the eggs sink to the bottom.

Bake the skillet for 40 to 45 minutes or until the middle is set and not runny.

If you're avoiding nightshades, substitute sweet potatoes for white.

TOTAL RECIPE MACRONUTRIENTS (IN GRAMS PER SERVING)	
PROTEIN	13G
FAT	14G
TOTAL CARB	18G
NET CARB	16G

CHAPTER THREE

PROTEIN-PACKED MEALS TO BUILD STRENGTH

When you come right down to it, protein is the structural molecule that we are all built on, and it's essential to your diet if you're putting your body to the test.

On the most basic level, proteins are made of chains of amino acids; the body breaks down protein and reassembles the amino acids into our cell membranes, our muscle and connective tissue, our enzymes and our hormones. Training in particular stresses and damages our tissues, and eating adequate dietary protein is important for repair and recovery. It's how we get stronger.

Eat protein as part of every balanced meal and in your pre- and post-workout snacks. Consume a variety of protein-dense sources such as animal muscle and organ meats, seafood and shellfish and eggs. Buy the best quality you can afford. If you use protein powders, treat them only as a supplement to your intake of real, whole-food sources.

TENDER ASIAN-MARINATED FLANK STEAK

ULTRA-TENDER BEEF WITH FLAVORS OF GINGER, GARLIC AND GREEN ONION

Flank steak is a really special piece of meat and when prepared well, it's melt-in-your-mouth tender. Because it can be somewhat tough, there are some tricks I use to make it more delicate, like marinating it for several hours to break down the tough fibers, cooking it at really high heat to sear it and lock in the juices and slicing it against the grain. Set it up to go the night before or in the morning before you leave for work, and all you'll have to do is cook it when you get home! Serve it on top of a tossed green salad with some avocado for a nourishing, complete meal.

MAKES 2 SERVINGS

1 lb (454 g) flank steak

2 garlic cloves, peeled and smashed

1" (2.5 cm) piece ginger, peeled and sliced into thin coins

3 green onions (2 oz [57 g]), white and light green parts, roughly chopped

¼ cup (59 mL) coconut aminos

2 tbsp (30 mL) lime juice

2 tsp (10 mL) dark sesame oil

1 tsp fish sauce

1 tbsp (15 mL) coconut oil

Combine all the ingredients except for the coconut oil in a plastic zip-top bag or a medium bowl. Cover and refrigerate for at least 2 hours. Longer is definitely better, up to 24 hours. Remove the meat and pat it dry. Discard the marinade.

Heat a skillet to medium-high heat and add the coconut oil. When it shimmers, add the steak, and sear for 3 minutes until a golden brown crust has formed. Flip the steak and sear the other side for 3 minutes. Then turn the heat down to medium-low and cook until it's to your preference, about 4 more minutes for medium.

Let rest on a cutting board for at least 5 minutes before slicing. Cut into thin strips, against the grain (muscle fibers). It'll be really tender that way.

Instead of pan-searing the steak, grill it.

TOTAL RECIPE MACRONUTRIENTS (IN GRAMS PER SERVING)

PROTEIN	45G
FAT	36G
TOTAL CARB	12G
NET CARB	11G

TEX-MEX DEVILED EGGS

A SMOKY, SPICY CHIPOTLE VERSION OF A CLASSIC

When I visited Austin for PaleoFX, I was so inspired by all the fantastic Tex-Mex flavors I saw on restaurant menus everywhere I ate. I came home and created a deviled egg in homage to my trip. Eggs are a great, inexpensive way to add protein to your diet, and hard-cooking a large batch on your weekly cook-up day gives you options throughout the week.

MAKES 3 SERVINGS

6 large eggs

¼ cup (59 mL) Creamy Olive Oil Mayo (page 206)

Zest of 1 lime

½ tsp + ½ tsp ground chipotle pepper

⅛ tsp sea salt

½ cup (9 g) pork rinds

1 tsp chopped chives

Start by hard-cooking the eggs. My tried-and-true method is to steam them because the shells slip right off. Place a medium pot on the stovetop, and fit it with a steamer basket. Fill the bottom of the pot with 1 inch/2.5 centimeters of water, then put the lid on and bring the water to a boil. Once the water boils, remove the eggs from the refrigerator, and place them in the steamer basket. Be careful: Steam can burn you! Replace the lid and steam the eggs for 10 minutes. Meanwhile, fill a medium bowl with water and several ice cubes. When your timer goes off, turn off the heat, and move the eggs to the ice water. Cool completely, then peel them.

While the eggs are cooling, combine the mayo, lime zest, ½ teaspoon chipotle pepper and salt in a medium bowl. Mix well to combine. Cut the peeled eggs in half lengthwise, and carefully remove the yolk. Add the yolks to the mayo mixture and stir very well, until everything is smooth. Spoon the filling back into the egg whites. Or if you're fancy, spoon the mixture into a plastic zip-top bag, cut off the corner and pipe it back in.

To prepare the topping, put the pork rinds and the rest of the chipotle pepper into a plastic zip-top bag, and seal it. Crush into crumbs with your hands. Sprinkle the deviled eggs with the chipotle pork rinds and chopped chives.

TOTAL RECIPE MACRONUTRIENTS (IN GRAMS PER SERVING)	
PROTEIN	37G
FAT	39G
TOTAL CARB	3G
NET CARB	3G

CURRIED CHICKEN SALAD

Growing up, we often ate chicken salad made from a leftover bird, and it was one of my favorite things to have for lunch. The grapes, celery and almonds give it a nice crunch, and the curry powder adds some spice. Homemade mayo is the healthy fat counterpoint to the protein from the chicken and keeps the salad from being dry. This recipe makes a large batch, which is perfect for leftovers or for feeding a group.

MAKES 8 SERVINGS

1 ½ lb (680 g) chicken breasts

1 tsp + 1 tsp sea salt

½ tsp black pepper

2 bay leaves

1" (2.5 cm) piece ginger, peeled and sliced into thin coins

1 cup (146 g) red grapes, halved

3 stalks celery (6 oz [170 g]), sliced diagonally

3 green onions (2 oz [57 g]), white and light green parts, thinly sliced

¼ cup (28 g) sliced almonds

½ tbsp (3 g) hot curry powder

¼ cup (59 mL) Creamy Olive Oil Mayo (page 206)

Begin by poaching the chicken. Lay the chicken breasts flat in a large, high-sided skillet or Dutch oven. Add 1 teaspoon salt, pepper, bay leaves and ginger. Add water until it covers the chicken by about 1 inch/2.5 centimeters. Cover the pan, and bring the water to a boil. Then reduce the heat to a simmer. Poach the chicken for about 15 minutes or until completely cooked through, then move it to a plate to cool. Once the chicken is cool enough to handle, dice it into small pieces.

Put the diced chicken, grapes, celery, green onions, almonds, curry powder and the rest of the salt in a large bowl. Stir everything well to combine. Then add the mayo and stir until everything is well-coated.

Use mild curry powder for a less spicy chicken salad.

TOTAL RECIPE MACRONUTRIENTS (IN GRAMS PER SERVING)	
PROTEIN	16G
FAT	15G
TOTAL CARB	6G
NET CARB	5G

SHRIMP AND SCALLOP CEVICHE

THE MEAL THAT COOKS ITSELF

In the summer months, firing up the oven sometimes isn't an option. When the temperature starts to climb, one of my favorite protein-rich main dishes is ceviche. It's cool because it uses the citrus fruit's acidity to "cook" the protein without heating it up. There are probably as many variations on this recipe as you can dream up, but this one is my favorite.

MAKES 4 SERVINGS

1 lb (454 g) raw shrimp, shelled and deveined

½ lb (227 g) raw scallops

½ jalapeño pepper, stem removed and finely chopped

1 medium avocado (5 oz [142 g]), pitted and diced

1 small mango, diced (about ½ cup [121 g])

Zest of 2 limes

Juice of 4 limes

Juice of 2 lemons

Juice of 2 oranges

Juice of 1 grapefruit

½ tsp sea salt

Chopped cilantro for garnish, optional

Dice the shrimp and scallops into small pieces. Combine everything in a large bowl and stir to combine. Cover and refrigerate for at least 6 hours or until the shrimp and scallops are no longer transparent. Garnish with cilantro if you'd like.

Substitute firm white-fleshed fish instead of shrimp or scallops.

TOTAL RECIPE MACRONUTRIENTS (IN GRAMS PER SERVING)	
PROTEIN	35G
FAT	10G
TOTAL CARB	38G
NET CARB	32G

APPLE FENNEL SLOW COOKER CHICKEN

THE EASIEST CHICKEN YOU'LL EVER MAKE

Using a slow cooker is one of the simplest ways to maximize your limited time in the kitchen. Add some protein, veggies, herbs and spices, and walk away. Couldn't be simpler. This slow cooker chicken is a staple in my household. Not only is it delicious and easy, but it's economical because whole chickens are more cost-effective than precut chicken parts.

MAKES 4 SERVINGS

½ medium fennel (4 oz [113 g]), sliced, fronds set aside

3 to 4 lb (1361 to 1814 g) whole chicken

1 tsp sea salt

½ tsp black pepper

½ red apple, sliced

Arrange the fennel fronds in the bottom of the slow cooker and place the chicken on top of them. Sprinkle half the salt and pepper in the cavity, then stuff it with apple and fennel. If there's extra apple and fennel, arrange it around the outside of the bird. Sprinkle the remaining salt and pepper on the outside of the chicken.

Cook the chicken on low for 5 hours or high for 3 hours.

After it's done cooking, put the chicken under the broiler on a baking tray to crisp the skin.

TOTAL RECIPE MACRONUTRIENTS (IN GRAMS PER SERVING)	
PROTEIN	43G
FAT	35G
TOTAL CARB	4G
NET CARB	3G

MOCHA-RUBBED SLOW COOKER POT ROAST

FORK-TENDER MEAT WITH EARTHY NOTES OF COFFEE AND COCOA

Confession time: I use the slow cooker far more than my oven for making roasts. Since the slow cooker minds itself, I can throw everything in it and head out to the gym while it does its thing. When I come home, I've got a delicious pile of protein waiting for dinner. As long as the meat has enough marbling, it'll come out tender and savory.

MAKES ABOUT 4 SERVINGS

FOR THE MOCHA RUB

2 tbsp (10 g) finely ground coffee

2 tbsp (30 g) smoked paprika

1 tbsp (15 g) black pepper

1 tbsp (7 g) cocoa powder

1 tsp Aleppo pepper

1 tsp chili powder

1 tsp ground ginger

1 tsp sea salt

FOR THE ROAST

2 lbs (907 g) beef pot roast

1 cup (237 mL) brewed coffee

1 cup (237 mL) beef broth

½ medium onion, chopped

6 dried black figs, chopped

3 tbsp (45 mL) balsamic vinegar

Sea salt and pepper, to taste

Prepare the mocha rub by mixing together the finely ground coffee, smoked paprika, black pepper, cocoa powder, Aleppo pepper, chili powder, ground ginger and salt in a small bowl. You won't use the entire batch if you're making a 2-pound/907 gram roast, so store the extra in an airtight container.

Pat the roast dry with a paper towel. Spoon 3 to 4 tablespoons/45 to 60 grams of the mocha rub mixture over the roast. Or place the roast and 3 to 4 tablespoons/45 to 60 grams of mocha rub in a plastic zip-top bag, seal and shake until it's evenly coated.

Combine the brewed coffee, beef broth, onion, figs and balsamic vinegar in a blender. Puree until liquefied. Pour the liquid into the slow cooker and place the roast gently on top. Cook on low for 5–6 hours.

Remove the meat from the slow cooker and shred it with two forks. You can boil the liquid in a pan until it reduces and thickens into a sauce. Or simply serve as is. Adjust seasonings with salt and pepper to taste.

Limiting caffeine? Use an extra cup/237 milliliters of beef broth, and omit the coffee.

TOTAL RECIPE MACRONUTRIENTS (IN GRAMS PER SERVING)	
PROTEIN	41G
FAT	37G
TOTAL CARB	37G
NET CARB	31G

SPICY MANGO AHI POKE

A FRESH PROTEIN-RICH TASTE OF HAWAII

I fell in love with poke (pronounced po-kee) some time ago for its simplicity. When I went to Hawaii and ate poke nearly every day, it rose to hall of fame status as one of my favorite dishes. Poke can be made with many different types of seafood, but my go-to is the classic ahi tuna. I've swapped out the soy sauce for coconut aminos and added orange for a contrast to the earthy sesame oil. My favorite way to eat poke is piled on top of fresh pork rinds for some crunch, but plantain chips work well, too.

MAKES 4 SERVINGS

1 lb (454 g) ahi tuna

½ cup (120 g) mango, diced

1 small avocado (5 oz [142 g]), diced

2 tbsp (30 mL) coconut aminos

4 tsp (20 mL) dark sesame oil

½ tbsp (7 g) sea salt

⅛ tsp black pepper

2 green onions, white and light green parts, thinly sliced for garnish

1 tsp sesame seeds, for garnish

Kicked Up Sriracha (page 216), for garnish

Cut the ahi into ½-inch/13-millimeter chunks. Combine all the ingredients except the green onions, sesame seeds and Sriracha, in a medium bowl and stir well to combine. Garnish with green onions, sesame seeds and Kicked Up Sriracha.

Use orange instead of mango.

TOTAL RECIPE MACRONUTRIENTS (IN GRAMS PER SERVING)	
PROTEIN	29G
FAT	19G
TOTAL CARB	21G
NET CARB	17G

LARB IN LETTUCE WRAPS

A DELICIOUSLY FLAVORED ASIAN CHICKEN DISH

The best way to describe larb—a Lao speciality—is to call it minced chicken with aromatics served in lettuce cups. It's one of my favorite ways to enjoy chicken breast that's moist and flavorful instead of dry, and once it's all prepared, it cooks in almost no time. To make it easier to prep, use a food processor to mince the meat finely. Serve it up in your lettuce of choice; butter (Boston) lettuce makes great cups, while romaine gives more of a boat style. Either way, it's delicious.

MAKES 4 SERVINGS

1 lb (454 g) chicken breasts, roughly chopped

3 green onions (2 oz [57 g]), white and light green parts, chopped

1 clove garlic, chopped

¼ cup (9 g) cilantro, packed

1" (2.5 cm) piece lemongrass, very finely chopped

½ serrano pepper (6 g), stem removed and chopped

1 tsp coconut aminos

1 tsp dark sesame oil

1 tsp fish sauce

1 tbsp (15 mL) coconut oil

1 head butter lettuce

Dark green parts of the green onions, sliced, for garnish

Place all the ingredients, except the coconut oil, lettuce and dark green parts of the green onions, in a food processor and pulse until the chicken is broken down into very small pieces.

Heat a large skillet over medium-high heat, and then add the coconut oil. Cook and stir the chicken, breaking up the chunks with a wooden spoon, for about 5 to 6 minutes or until it's no longer pink.

Serve in a bowl with lettuce leaves on the side for wrapping it up. Garnish with green onions.

Mix 1 teaspoon Kicked Up Sriracha (page 216) with 3 tablespoons/ 45 milliliters Creamy Olive Oil Mayo (page 206) for a topping.

TOTAL RECIPE MACRONUTRIENTS (IN GRAMS PER SERVING)	
PROTEIN	20G
FAT	13G
TOTAL CARB	8G
NET CARB	7G

HONEY GARLIC LEMON CHICKEN WINGS

SO GOOD, YOU'LL PROBABLY WANT TO MAKE A DOUBLE BATCH

When I say these wings are finger-lickin' good, it's not an overstatement. During recipe development, I brought a couple of batches to the gym for taste-testing, and they were a huge hit. In this recipe, the honey balances out the tang from the lemon, the buttery ghee and the spicy cayenne. It's a pretty small amount in the grand scheme of a performance-based diet, so don't have any hesitations about using it in this application. The right amount of sweetness really makes the glaze sing!

MAKES 3 SERVINGS

FOR THE WINGS

1 ½ lb (680 g) chicken wings

1 tbsp (15 mL) melted ghee

½ tsp garlic powder

½ tsp sea salt

¼ tsp black pepper

FOR THE GLAZE

1 tbsp (15 g) ghee

5 cloves garlic, finely chopped

Zest of 1 lemon

2 tbsp (30 mL) lemon juice

1 ½ tbsp (23 mL) raw honey

Pinch of cayenne pepper

Preheat the oven to 400°F/204°C and line a baking sheet with foil or parchment paper. Pat the wings dry with a paper towel and put them on the baking sheet. Drizzle with the melted ghee, then sprinkle with the garlic powder, salt and pepper. Toss well with your hands to combine, then arrange them in a single layer. Bake the wings for 30 minutes or until crispy and golden. Put them in a medium bowl to cool a bit.

Prepare the glaze next. In a small saucepan, combine the ghee, garlic, lemon zest and juice, honey and cayenne pepper. Bring the mixture to a boil then reduce to a simmer, cooking until the mixture has reduced by about half. Be careful not to walk away because this can burn quickly! Immediately pour the glaze onto the wings, and toss them until they're nice and coated.

TOTAL RECIPE MACRONUTRIENTS (IN GRAMS PER SERVING)	
PROTEIN	23G
FAT	24G
TOTAL CARB	12G
NET CARB	12G

ROASTED CHICKEN AND ASPARAGUS SALAD

Salads like this are the quintessential lunch or simple dinner dish, and they get better as they sit for a day or two because the flavors meld. It's really the perfect bite, with plenty of protein from the chicken, some carbs from the veggies and healthy fats from the olive oil mayo. To keep it from feeling too heavy, the dill, parsley and lemon juice lighten things up. One more reason to love asparagus other than its fresh flavor: It's particularly rich in the antioxidant glutathione, which helps neutralize cell-damaging free radicals.

MAKES 4 SERVINGS

1 lb (454 g) asparagus

1 medium red onion, thinly sliced

1 tbsp (15 mL) avocado oil

½ tsp sea salt

1 lb (454 g) chicken breasts, poached and shredded

2 oz (57 g) snap peas, stemmed and halved

1 garlic clove, finely chopped

1 tsp dried dill

¼ cup (2 oz [57g]) chopped fresh parsley

1 tbsp (15 mL) lemon juice

¼ tsp sea salt

¼ tsp black pepper

2 tbsp (30 mL) Creamy Olive Oil Mayo (page 206)

Preheat the oven to 400°F/204°C, and line a baking sheet with foil or parchment paper. Trim the bottom third off the asparagus spears and lay them on the sheet with the red onion. Drizzle with avocado oil and sprinkle with salt, then toss with your hands until it's combined. Roast for 20 to 25 minutes or until the veggies are lightly brown and caramelized. Set aside.

While the veggies are roasting, prepare the rest of the salad. In a large bowl, mix the shredded chicken, snap peas, garlic, dill, parsley, lemon juice, salt and pepper. Stir to combine. When the veggies are done, mix them into the salad, then stir in the mayo until everything is lightly coated. Serve cold.

Grill the chicken instead of poaching it.

TOTAL RECIPE MACRONUTRIENTS (IN GRAMS PER SERVING)	
PROTEIN	21G
FAT	18G
TOTAL CARB	8G
NET CARB	5G

TENDER BRAISED BONELESS BEEF SHORT RIBS

TENDER, SAVORY SHORT RIBS WITH A SURPRISE INGREDIENT

These are probably the best short ribs I've ever eaten, though I may be a bit biased. There's something about this dish that has a rich, comfort-food feel with just a few ingredients. Using ground shiitake mushrooms to create a layer of umami (savory) flavor is the key to the lip-smacking goodness, and the apple cider vinegar helps tenderize the meat. If you can find 2 pounds (900 g) of boneless short ribs, these are worth a double batch.

MAKES 3 SERVINGS

1 tsp + 2 tbsp (30 g) ghee

1 oz (28 g) dried, ground shiitake mushrooms

1 medium sweet onion, thinly sliced

¼ tsp sea salt

1 lb (454 g) boneless beef short ribs

2 tbsp (30 mL) apple cider vinegar

½ cup (118 mL) chicken broth

Preheat the oven to 325°F/163°C, and grease a 7-inch x 7-inch/18-centimeter x 18-centimeter covered casserole dish with 1 teaspoon ghee. To make the shiitake mushroom powder, add the dried shiitakes to a food processor or high-powered blender; process until they're broken down and powdery. Move to an airtight container, keeping 2 teaspoons/10 grams reserved for the recipe.

Now sear the meat. In a large skillet over medium-high heat, brown the onion in 1 tablespoon/15 grams ghee and the salt. Move these to the baking dish. Add another tablespoon/15 grams ghee, then sear the meat, about 3 minutes per side. You're looking for a nice caramelized crust to form. The best way to get it is to not move the meat once you lay it down in the pan until it's ready to flip. Remove the meat, and place it in the baking dish. Immediately add the apple cider vinegar and chicken broth to the pan, scraping up any browned bits. Turn off the heat.

Dust both sides of the meat with the ground shiitakes. Nestle the short ribs in between the onion in the baking dish, then carefully pour the vinegar and broth mixture around the meat. Bake for 75 minutes, covered, then remove the lid and bake for another 30 minutes.

TOTAL RECIPE MACRONUTRIENTS (IN GRAMS PER SERVING)

PROTEIN	24G
FAT	66G
TOTAL CARB	11G
NET CARB	9G

EGGPLANT AND SAUSAGE STACKS

SAVORY STACKS OF EGGPLANT, SAUSAGE AND SIMPLE HOMEMADE SAUCE

While this recipe at first glance looks complex, it's really pretty easy to do. If you want to minimize prep time, you can make a batch or two of sauce ahead of time and freeze it. Then thaw the sauce on the day you want to make it, bake the eggplant and brown the sausage. If you're really pressed for time, slice the roasted eggplant into ribbons, then toss it in a bowl with the sauce and sausage, lazy-style! Eggplant is a good source of B vitamins and trace minerals, like copper and manganese.

MAKES 4 SERVINGS

FOR THE HOMEMADE TOMATO SAUCE

1 tbsp (15 mL) olive oil

6 cloves garlic, finely chopped

1 can (28 oz [794 g]) whole peeled tomatoes

1 can (15 oz [425 g]) crushed tomatoes

1 tbsp (2 g) dried Italian herbs

1 tsp sea salt

FOR THE STACKS

2 lb (907 g) eggplant, cut into ⅓" (0.8 cm) slices

2 tsp (10 g) sea salt

2 tsp (6 g) black pepper

2 tsp (4 g) onion powder

3 tbsp (45 mL) + 1 tbsp (15 mL) avocado oil

1 lb (454 g) Italian sausage

½ oz (14 g) fresh basil leaves, optional

Start by making the sauce. Warm the olive oil in a large pot over medium heat. Add the garlic. Cook and stir for about 30 seconds until the garlic starts to smell awesome. Add the peeled tomatoes, breaking them up into small chunks with a wooden spoon, then add the crushed tomatoes, Italian herbs and salt. Cover, lid cracked to release steam, and bring to a boil. Reduce to a simmer and cook for about 60 minutes.

Preheat the oven to 400°F/204°C. Line two baking sheets with parchment paper and arrange the eggplant slices so they're in one layer. Combine the salt, pepper and onion powder in a small bowl and mix. Lightly brush the eggplant with 3 tablespoons/45 milliliters avocado oil, then sprinkle with half the seasoning. Flip the slices over and repeat. Bake for 25 to 30 minutes or until the eggplant is soft and lightly brown. Remove from the oven and set aside.

While the eggplant bakes, get the sausage ready. Heat a large skillet over medium-high heat and add 1 tablespoon/15 milliliters avocado oil. Empty the sausage from its casing and use a wooden spoon to break it up into small pieces. Cook and stir for about 8 minutes or until the sausage is cooked through and browned.

Assemble the stacks this way: Place a piece of eggplant down on a plate. Next add sauce, sausage and a basil leaf or two. Top with another piece of eggplant and a spoonful of sauce. Repeat until you've used up all the eggplant.

TOTAL RECIPE MACRONUTRIENTS (IN GRAMS PER SERVING)	
PROTEIN	19G
FAT	53G
TOTAL CARB	18G
NET CARB	12G

PULLED PORK AND SWEET POTATO HASH

AN EGG-FREE BREAKFAST STAPLE

This is one of the all-time most popular recipes in my household for several reasons. It's egg-free, so if you need to avoid them for some reason, this is still an awesome first meal option. Of course, you can always add eggs on the side to bump up the protein and healthy fat profile. It also doubles as a great post-workout nosh, and it can serve as a basic template for so many flavor combinations. The sweet potatoes provide lots of nutrient-dense carbohydrate, and the pulled pork gives it a protein punch.

MAKES 6 SERVINGS

FOR THE PULLED PORK

2 lb (907 g) boneless pork, shoulder roast or Boston butt roast

½ tbsp (8 g) sea salt

FOR THE HASH

1 ½ lb (680 g) sweet potatoes, peeled and grated

2 tbsp (30 g) ghee

1 medium onion, diced

¼ tsp + ½ tsp sea salt

½ tsp black pepper

6 eggs, optional

The day before you plan to eat this, start the pulled pork. Place the shoulder roast in the slow cooker, and rub it all over with ½ tablespoon/8 grams salt. Cover and turn the heat on low for 12 to 14 hours. When the time is up, move the meat to a large bowl and shred it with two forks. Set aside or refrigerate until you make the hash. The day before, I also grate the sweet potatoes and let them sit, uncovered, in the refrigerator. This dries the potatoes out and makes it easier for the hash to brown.

Make the hash. Heat a very large skillet over medium-high heat and melt 1 tablespoon/ 15 grams ghee in the pan. Cook and stir the onions with ¼ teaspoon salt until softened and slightly brown, about 5 minutes. Add the sweet potatoes, then add another tablespoon/15 grams ghee and ½ teaspoon more salt. Allow the bottom of the sweet potatoes to brown over medium-high heat for about 5 minutes. Then flip in sections with a spatula and let the other side brown, another 3 to 4 minutes. Turn off the heat and mix in the pulled pork.

Form wells in the hash with a spoon and crack eggs into them. Cover the pan so the eggs steam through.

TOTAL RECIPE MACRONUTRIENTS (IN GRAMS PER SERVING)	
PROTEIN	37G
FAT	22G
TOTAL CARB	22G
NET CARB	21G

BADASS BOWL

This recipe was inspired by my former love of layered burrito bowls, and it's got all the flavor with cleaner ingredients and lots of protein. The base of the bowl is cauliflower rice and spiced ground meat—beef or turkey are great, though just about any meat will work. Get creative with your own favorite toppings or whip up some Awesomesauce (page 210) and dollop it on top with chopped lettuce or cilantro. This is a great recipe to double and eat as leftovers!

MAKES 4 SERVINGS

¾ tsp sea salt

½ tsp black pepper

½ tsp ground coriander

½ tsp garlic powder

½ tsp dried oregano

½ tsp cumin

½ tsp ground chipotle pepper

1 tbsp (15 mL) coconut oil

1 lb (454 g) ground beef or turkey

Savory Cauliflower Rice (page 174)

1 cup (237 mL) Awesomesauce (page 210)

Chopped romaine lettuce or chopped cilantro for garnish

In a small bowl, combine the salt and all the spices and mix. Heat a large skillet over medium-high heat and add the coconut oil. Add the meat and the spices, then cook and stir, breaking the meat up with a wooden spoon until it browns, about 6 to 8 minutes.

Serve this up in a bowl by layering the cauliflower rice at the bottom and the meat on top. Top with Awesomesauce and chopped lettuce or cilantro.

Substitute cooked white rice for cauliflower rice to bump up the carb content for a great post-workout meal.

TOTAL RECIPE MACRONUTRIENTS (IN GRAMS PER SERVING)

PROTEIN	29G
FAT	46G
TOTAL CARB	14G
NET CARB	8G

KOREAN BIBIMBAP

UNEXPECTED COMFORT FOOD AT ITS BEST

There are many different variations of bibimbap, and my Paleo interpretation has ground beef, cauliflower rice and raw and cooked veggies. If you're trying to bump up the carbohydrate content, substitute white rice for the cauliflower rice. If I'm not pressed for time, I arrange all the components on top of the meat and cauliflower rice base because the presentation is really quite stunning. After all, we eat with our eyes first!

MAKES 4 SERVINGS

1 lb (454 g) ground beef

2 tsp (10 mL) coconut oil

2 cloves garlic, finely chopped

1" (2.5 cm) piece of ginger, peeled and finely chopped

1 tbsp (15 mL) coconut aminos

½ tsp fish sauce

3 tbsp (45 mL) coconut oil, divided

½ lb (227 g) brown mushrooms, sliced

¼ tsp sea salt

1 large bunch spinach (5 cups [150 g] packed), stems trimmed off

4 large eggs or pastured egg yolks

Savory Cauliflower Rice (page 174)

2 tsp (10 mL) dark sesame oil

¼ lb (113 g) daikon radish, grated or julienned

¼ lb (113 g) carrots, grated or julienned

Get the ground beef going. Heat a large skillet over medium-high heat, then add 2 teaspoons/10 milliliters coconut oil. Cook and stir the beef, breaking it up with a wooden spoon, until it's browned and cooked through, about 6 to 8 minutes. If the beef is really fatty, you may want to drain off some of the grease. If not, just add about half the garlic, the ginger, the coconut aminos and the fish sauce, and heat for another minute. Move the beef to a medium bowl.

Now you'll get the veggies cooked. I do this in the same pan, one after the other, since they cook quickly. Keep the skillet on medium-high heat. Add 1 tablespoon/15 milliliters of coconut oil, then the sliced mushrooms and salt. Cook and stir the mushrooms for about 5 minutes, until they begin to brown and they've lost some of their moisture. Move the mushrooms to a small bowl. Add a tablespoon/15 milliliters of coconut oil to the skillet and the other half of the garlic. Cook for about 30 seconds, then add the spinach. Stir for another 2 minutes or until the spinach is wilted but not mushy. Move to a small bowl.

The last step will be to fry the eggs. Heat the same skillet over medium-high, then add the last tablespoon/15 milliliters coconut oil. Crack the eggs into the pan and fry them for about 30 seconds. Reduce the heat to medium-low and cook until the egg whites are no longer clear, about 3 to 4 minutes.

Construct your bibimbap: cauliflower rice goes on the bottom with ground beef on top of that, then drizzle with ½ teaspoon dark sesame oil. Top each bowl with a small amount of spinach, mushrooms, daikon and carrots, then an egg. Serve with hot chili sauce if you like some spice.

Instead of frying the egg, you can serve raw pastured egg yolk on top of the bowl.

TOTAL RECIPE MACRONUTRIENTS (IN GRAMS PER SERVING)	
PROTEIN	32G
FAT	52G
TOTAL CARB	21G
NET CARB	13G

LEMON ARTICHOKE CHICKEN

JUICY CHICKEN BREAST IS NOT A MYTH

Chicken breast is one of the most ubiquitous, easily available, lean and palatable protein sources out there, but it's notorious for being drier than the Sahara when cooked. I took my foolproof method for always-juicy chicken breast and bumped up the flavor with artichoke hearts, capers, garlic and red pepper flakes. This recipe yields a two-pound (907 g) batch, perfect for leftovers during a busy training week.

MAKES 6 SERVINGS

2 lb (907 g) chicken breasts

Zest of 2 lemons

6 tbsp (90 mL) lemon juice

1 tsp sea salt

½ tsp black pepper

1 tbsp (15 g) ghee

½ cup (118 mL) chicken broth

1 tsp arrowroot flour

1 can (14 oz [396 g]) artichoke hearts, chopped

2 cloves garlic, finely chopped

2 tbsp (17 g) capers

¼ tsp red pepper flakes

First, get the meat ready to marinate. Place the chicken breasts in a plastic zip-top bag or between two sheets of waxed paper and pound with a meat mallet until it's ½ inch/ 13 millimeters thick. You may have to do this in two or three batches. When all the chicken is pounded out, add it to a large zip-top bag with the lemon zest, lemon juice, salt and pepper. Marinate for at least 30 minutes in the refrigerator.

Heat a large skillet over medium-high heat, then add the ghee. Fry the chicken for 4 to 5 minutes per side, until it's caramelized and brown on each side. Move the chicken to a plate, and add the chicken broth to the pan, scraping up all the browned bits. Add the arrowroot flour, artichokes, garlic, capers and red pepper flakes. Bring the broth to a boil so the mixture thickens. Adjust the seasoning with salt and pepper if needed, then pour over the chicken.

TIP: Don't disturb the meat in the pan until you're ready to flip. It'll release cleanly when it's ready. I like to let the meat rest on a cutting board for 10 minutes, then slice it.

TOTAL RECIPE MACRONUTRIENTS (IN GRAMS PER SERVING)	
PROTEIN	26G
FAT	14G
TOTAL CARB	4G
NET CARB	3G

GREEK BURGER SALAD

BURGER MEETS SALAD WITH A TASTE OF GREECE

The concept of this meal couldn't be much easier: Make savory, spiced lamb patties and serve them atop a salad with fresh veggies and a simple drizzle of lemon juice and olive oil. When it's the thick of summer, salads are my go-to dinner choice, and I find myself making this combination a lot. Lamb is an oft-forgotten red meat that's a great beef alternative. It's high in B vitamins and is a good source of iron and other trace minerals. Since most lamb is grass-fed, it comes with similar fat profile benefits to beef.

MAKES 4 SERVINGS

FOR THE BURGERS

1 lb (454 g) ground lamb

1 tbsp (15 mL) water

¼ tsp cream of tartar

½ tsp sea salt

⅛ tsp baking soda

1 tsp garlic powder

1 tsp dried oregano

½ tsp onion powder

½ tsp ground coriander

¼ tsp black pepper

1 tbsp (15 mL) coconut oil

FOR THE SALAD

1 large head romaine lettuce (8 oz [227 g]), chopped

¼ cup (4 g) mint leaves, packed

¼ red onion, thinly sliced

½ medium cucumber (8 oz [227 g]), peeled and thinly sliced

½ cup (2 oz [64 g]) pitted black olives

½ cup (3 oz [85 g]) cherry tomatoes, halved

1 tbsp (15 mL) olive oil

1 tbsp (15 mL) lemon juice

Mint Basil Brazil Nut Pesto (page 202), optional

Start by making the burgers. Place the ground lamb in a large bowl. In a small bowl, mix the water, cream of tartar and baking soda with a spoon. Pour this onto the ground lamb. Let it sit for 5 minutes, then add the salt and spices. Mix the lamb and seasonings with your hands until combined but not overworked. At this point, take a small pinch of the meat, and fry it in the skillet to check the seasoning level. If it needs more salt and pepper, add it now. Shape the meat into 4 patties. A dimple pressed into the top of the burger will keep it flat during cooking.

Heat a large skillet over medium-high heat, and add the coconut oil. Fry the burgers for 4 to 5 minutes on each side. Remove to a plate while you make the salad.

For the salad, arrange the romaine and mint leaves as the base, then add the red onion, cucumber, black olives and cherry tomatoes on top. Drizzle with olive oil and lemon juice, then lay the burgers on top. Serve with Mint Basil Brazil Nut Pesto for dipping.

To save time, mix the seasonings with the lamb and fry it as ground meat, not as patties. It'll save a step, and it's just as delicious.

TOTAL RECIPE MACRONUTRIENTS (IN GRAMS PER SERVING)	
PROTEIN	25G
FAT	62G
TOTAL CARB	13G
NET CARB	7G

GARLIC LEMON SHRIMP WITH CAULIFLOWER GRITS

A GRAIN-FREE TWIST ON A CLASSIC SOUTHERN FAVORITE

Grits are a staple in Southern cuisine, but they're made from corn, a grain typically avoided in a Paleo template. Here, I've subbed the grits for cauliflower, which is chopped finely and cooked down in a savory broth to create a soft, creamy texture. The cauliflower grits would be equally as delicious served with blackened chicken on top.

MAKES 4 SERVINGS

FOR THE CAULIFLOWER GRITS

1 small head (20 oz [567 g]) cauliflower, cut into florets

1 tbsp (15 g) ghee

½ large onion, diced

1 ½ cups (355 mL) chicken broth

½ cup (118 mL) full-fat coconut milk

¼ tsp sea salt

¼ tsp black pepper

FOR THE GARLIC LEMON SHRIMP

1 lb (454 g) shrimp, peeled and deveined

Zest of 2 lemons

½ tsp garlic powder

⅛ tsp sea salt

⅛ tsp black pepper

2 tsp (10 g) ghee

1 tbsp (15 mL) lemon juice

Chopped parsley for garnish

The best way to rice cauliflower is in a food processor fitted with a shredding or grating blade. It can also be done with a regular blade by adding the cauliflower in a few batches, and pulsing it into small pieces the size of rice.

Heat a medium pot over medium heat, then add the ghee and onion. Cook and stir for about 4 minutes, until the onion begins to brown. Add the cauliflower, chicken broth, coconut milk, salt and pepper. Turn up the heat to high and bring the mixture to a boil, then reduce the heat to a simmer. Cook, uncovered, for 30 to 35 minutes or until the cauliflower is very soft and most of the liquid has cooked off.

Pat the shrimp dry with a paper towel and sprinkle it with lemon zest, garlic powder, salt and pepper. Toss to make sure it's very well coated. Heat a large skillet over medium-high heat, then add the ghee. Place the shrimp in the skillet in a single layer, and cook for 1 minute on each side or until they're no longer pink and are light golden brown.

Serve the shrimp on top of the cauliflower grits, add a drizzle of lemon juice and chopped parsley as garnish.

Serve the garlic lemon shrimp on cooked rice instead of the cauliflower grits to bump up the carbohydrate content.

TOTAL RECIPE MACRONUTRIENTS (IN GRAMS PER SERVING)	
PROTEIN	26G
FAT	15G
TOTAL CARB	7G
NET CARB	5G

BLACKENED FISH SOFT TACOS WITH MANGO SLAW

BECAUSE EVEN PALEO FOLKS NEED TACO TUESDAY

Who knows exactly when or where Taco Tuesday originated, but it's safe to say it's a delicious tradition. Here, whitefish—which cooks quickly—is rubbed with blackening seasoning and served with a flavor-packed simple slaw and, if you're feeling fancy, Roasted Poblano Sauce. It'd be quite tasty on a plate all by itself, but when wrapped in a Five-Minute Tortilla, this combo really shines.

MAKES 4 SERVINGS

1 lb (454 g) firm whitefish such as cod, cut into 1" (2.5 cm) strips

2 tbsp (12 g) Blackening Dust (page xx)

3 cups (210 g) shredded green or Savoy cabbage

½ cup (120 g) mango, sliced

¼ cup (4 g) cilantro, chopped

2 tsp (10 mL) lime juice

2 tbsp (30 mL) avocado oil

¼ tsp sea salt

⅛ tsp black pepper

1 tbsp (15 mL) coconut oil

Five-Minute Tortillas (page 125)

Roasted Poblano Sauce (page 215)

Toss the fish with the Blackening Dust until it's well coated. Set aside. In a large bowl, combine the cabbage, mango, cilantro, lime juice, avocado oil, salt and pepper. Mix until everything is combined and set aside.

Heat a large skillet over medium-high heat, and add the coconut oil. Sear the fish about 1 minute on each side; it cooks fast.

Assemble the tacos: Place the fish in the tortilla, then top with the slaw and some Roasted Poblano Sauce.

You can substitute shrimp for fish if you'd like.

TOTAL RECIPE MACRONUTRIENTS (IN GRAMS PER SERVING)	
PROTEIN	28G
FAT	41G
TOTAL CARB	26G
NET CARB	23G

PANFRIED STEAK WITH MUSHROOM SHALLOT JUS

THE PERFECT STEAK, EVERY TIME

Knowing how to panfry the perfect steak is a trick all home cooks need up their sleeve. The secret is a well-seasoned piece of meat seared off in ghee—which has a high smoke point—using a cast-iron skillet. I use this method often since I don't have a grill, and sometimes I just skip the mushroom jus if I'm pressed for time. But, if you have a few extra minutes, it adds great depth of flavor that compliments the steak well.

MAKES 1 OR 2 SERVINGS

½ lb (227 g) grass-fed New York strip steak

¼ tsp + ¼ tsp sea salt

⅛ tsp black pepper

1 tbsp (15 g) ghee

½ lb (227 g) sliced brown mushrooms

1 medium shallot, thinly sliced

⅓ cup (79 mL) chicken broth

½ tsp arrowroot flour

Keep the steak out at room temperature for 15 to 30 minutes. Season both sides of the steak with ¼ teaspoon salt and pepper. Heat a large skillet over medium-high heat and melt the ghee. Add the steak and sear one side for about 4 minutes, then flip and sear the other side for about 2 minutes for medium rare, 3 minutes for medium. Remove to a cutting board, and let it rest while you prepare the rest of the dish.

In the same skillet over medium-high heat, add the mushrooms, shallot and ¼ teaspoon salt. Cook and stir for about 6 minutes or until the mushrooms have softened and the shallot begins to brown. Add the chicken broth and turn off the heat, then stir in the arrowroot flour so the liquid thickens a bit. Adjust the seasoning with salt and pepper, if needed.

TOTAL RECIPE MACRONUTRIENTS (IN GRAMS PER SERVING)

PROTEIN	19G
FAT	27G
TOTAL CARB	6G
NET CARB	5G

PROSCIUTTO-WRAPPED SALMON WITH HONEY LEMON GLAZE

ÜBER-SOPHISTICATED BUT ÜBER-SIMPLE

Sometimes even though you're trying to keep food basic, you still want it to taste amazing. After all, boring meals day in and out turn eating—and cooking—from a fun experience into a chore. The inspiration for this dish happened when I was looking for a way to keep oven-baked salmon from drying out. By wrapping it in prosciutto, it stays moist and the honey lemon glaze is a nice counterpoint to the salty cured meat. Salmon is one of the simplest ways to add anti-inflammatory Omega-3 fatty acids to your plate.

MAKES 3 TO 4 SERVINGS

FOR THE SALMON

1 lb (454 g) salmon, skinned and cut into 2" (5.1 cm) slices

½ tsp black pepper

3 oz (85 g) sliced prosciutto

FOR THE GLAZE

1 tbsp (15 g) ghee

1 ½ tbsp (23 mL) raw honey

Zest of 1 lemon

2 tbsp (30 mL) lemon juice

Preheat the oven to 350°F/177°C and line a baking sheet with foil or parchment paper.

Remove any pin bones from the salmon and sprinkle the slices with pepper. Cut the prosciutto slices in half lengthwise, then wrap each slice of salmon with the prosciutto. Bake about 10 to 12 minutes or until the salmon is cooked through but not overdone.

Meanwhile, make the glaze. Combine the ghee, honey, lemon zest and lemon juice in a small pot and stir to combine. Bring the mixture to a boil, then lower the heat to a simmer. Cook until the glaze reduces by about half. This can burn easily so keep an eye on it.

When the salmon is done, remove it from the oven and spoon the glaze on top. Serve the extra glaze on the side for dipping.

TOTAL RECIPE MACRONUTRIENTS (IN GRAMS PER SERVING)	
PROTEIN	29G
FAT	9G
TOTAL CARB	3G
NET CARB	3G

SLOW COOKER LAMB SHANKS WITH ROOT VEGGIES

SATISFYING, CARB-DENSE ROOT VEGGIES MEET FALL-APART-TENDER LAMB

Slow cookers are a must for busy people, and this method for preparing lamb shanks is a winner. As the lamb cooks, it gets so tender it falls off the bone and creates a savory gravy that thickens as the root veggies break down and soften. I added chicken broth and Dijon mustard to deepen the flavor. The combination of root veggies ups the carbohydrate content of the meal, and you can swap celery root for turnip or parsnip depending on what's available.

MAKES 4 TO 6 SERVINGS

4 lb (1814 g) lamb shanks

2 tsp (10 g) sea salt

1 tsp black pepper

2 tbsp (30 g) ghee

4 cloves garlic, peeled and smashed

2 sprigs (14 g) rosemary

4 sprigs (1 g) thyme

2 large carrots (8 oz [227 g]) carrots, chopped

1 medium celery root (16 oz [454 g]), peeled and diced

1 large onion, (16 oz [454 g]), chopped

1 lb (454 g) Yukon gold potatoes, peeled and chopped

½ cup (118 mL) chicken broth

1 tbsp (15 mL) Dijon mustard

For the best flavor, sear the lamb shanks before putting them in the slow cooker. To do that, dry the lamb with a paper towel, then season the shanks with salt and pepper. Heat a large skillet over high heat, and add 1 tablespoon/15 grams ghee. Sear the lamb shanks until they develop a nice brown crust, about 3 to 4 minutes per side. Place the shanks in the slow cooker and lay the garlic, rosemary and thyme sprigs on top of the meat.

Put another tablespoon/15 grams ghee in the same skillet. Add the carrots, celery root, onion and potatoes. Cook and stir over medium-high heat about 3 or 4 minutes, or until the veggies start to caramelize. Pour the veggies on top of the lamb in the slow cooker.

Immediately return the pan to the heat, and pour in the chicken broth to deglaze the pan, scraping up all the brown bits. Stir in the Dijon mustard, and pour this mixture over the veggies and lamb in the slow cooker.

Cook for 5 hours on high or 8 hours on low, stirring 2 or 3 times during cooking.

Substitute parsnip or turnip for the potatoes if you'd like to lessen your carb intake.

TOTAL RECIPE MACRONUTRIENTS (IN GRAMS PER SERVING)	
PROTEIN	48G
FAT	38G
TOTAL CARB	22G
NET CARB	18G

SPICED PORK TENDERLOIN WITH ROASTED PLUM SAUCE

Pork tenderloin is a great, relatively inexpensive way to incorporate lean protein into your diet. Soaking the meat in a brine—essentially a salty, spiced water bath—imparts both flavor and extra tenderness. Even though this cut of pork is notoriously tender, it's also very lean and can dry out quickly when cooked. I paired this with a sweet and tangy sauce made from plums, which are roasted to concentrate the flavor.

MAKES 2 TO 3 SERVINGS

FOR THE BRINE

2 tbsp (30 g) sea salt

1 tsp anise seed

1 tsp coriander seed

½ tsp black peppercorns

½ tsp red pepper flakes

½ cup (118 mL) apple cider vinegar

2 ½ cups (591 mL) water

FOR THE PORK

1 lb (454 g) pork tenderloin

1 ½ lb (680 g) black plums, pitted and halved

2 tsp (10 mL) melted ghee

⅛ tsp sea salt

⅛ tsp black pepper

½ tsp ground ginger

⅛ tsp ground coriander

1 tbsp (15 g) ghee

Brine the pork at least 2 hours in advance. In a large plastic zip-top bag, combine the salt, anise, coriander, peppercorns, red pepper flakes, apple cider vinegar and water. Add the pork tenderloin to the brine, and refrigerate for two to three hours.

Preheat the oven to 325°F/163°C, and line a baking sheet with foil or parchment paper. Place the halved plums on the sheet, then drizzle with melted ghee and sprinkle with salt and pepper. Roast the plums for about 30 minutes or until they're soft. Remove them from the oven, and let cool. Scrape the flesh from the skins—they can be bitter—into a medium bowl. Use a fork to lightly mash the plums into a sauce.

Remove the pork from its brine. Discard the brine and pat the tenderloin dry with a paper towel. Line the baking sheet with fresh foil or parchment. Rub the pork with the ginger and coriander. Sear the pork in a skillet over high heat in 1 tablespoon/15 grams of ghee for 3 minutes per side. Then put the pork on the baking sheet. Roast the meat at 325°F/163°C for about 20 minutes or until the pork is cooked through and the juices run clear. It's best to use a meat thermometer to test if the tenderloin is done and prevent overcooking.

TOTAL RECIPE MACRONUTRIENTS (IN GRAMS PER SERVING)	
PROTEIN	34G
FAT	14G
TOTAL CARB	33G
NET CARB	31G

CHAPTER FOUR

CARB-DENSE SIDES TO MAXIMIZE RECOVERY

Carbohydrates are probably the most misunderstood of the macronutrients. Their primary and essential function is to provide energy. But when eaten in excess—including the processed, refined grains and sugars typical in Western diets—issues often arise. Therefore, grains and excess sugars are not part of basic Paleo templates. Finding a balance of carb intake to support training and the replenishment of energy stores, while avoiding the problems associated with grains and refined sugars, is critical.

Including lots of vegetables—both starchy and green—and some fruit is the best way to keep your carb intake in the sweet spot. When training hard, eating a big whack of carbohydrate and protein after your workout is key to speed replenishment of fuel spent and to get recovery going. If you find your training becoming sluggish, check in with your daily carb intake, and perhaps increase it a bit. Training on inadequate carbohydrates is only survivable for so long.

In this book, you'll find some carb sources that break from what some Paleo templates recommend—in particular, white potatoes and white rice. These two sources of dense, starchy carbohydrates present refuel options appropriate for the performance-minded crowd and might not be appropriate for all who are eating a Paleo diet. In particular, if you're still working on optimizing blood sugar management or you have issues with nightshades, avoid white potatoes. White rice, though technically a grain, is devoid of gluten and is considered a safe starch by many. Test these sources in your diet, and if they don't work, it's fine to avoid them.

To build a balanced plate at mealtime, combine the recipes in this chapter with those in the Protein-Packed Meals to Build Strength chapter and add some extra green veggies or fruit plus some healthy fat.

BAKED YUCA FRIES

THE EASIEST WAY TO COOK YUCA

When it comes to carb-density in a vegetable, yuca is where it's at. Whether it's called yuca, manioc, tapioca or cassava, it's all the same. Prepared yuca can take many forms, and in many cultures, it's boiled and made into a mash. The only catch is that it gets very sticky and tough to work with. After attempting several other yuca recipes for this book, I decided to include this one because it's so simple and takes no special equipment or a preponderance of patience to make.

MAKES 3 OR 4 SERVINGS

2 lb (907 g) yuca, peeled

2 tbsp (30 mL) melted ghee

1 tsp smoked paprika

1 tsp onion powder

1 tsp sea salt

½ tsp black pepper

Preheat the oven to 400°F/204°C and line two baking sheets with foil or parchment paper.

Cut the yuca into pieces the size of steak fries. If you make them too thin, they'll get dried out and hard. Divide the yuca up onto the two sheets. Drizzle the yuca with melted ghee and sprinkle it with the spices and salt. Toss everything until it's well coated.

Bake the yuca for 20 to 25 minutes or until the pieces are tender inside and lightly brown on the edges, but not burnt. I like to stir them at least once during baking so they brown evenly.

TOTAL RECIPE MACRONUTRIENTS (IN GRAMS PER SERVING)	
PROTEIN	3G
FAT	8G
TOTAL CARB	87G
NET CARB	83G

BAKED CINNAMON CARROTS

AN UNEXPECTED WAY TO MAKE CARROTS DELICIOUS

The humble carrot is a great root veggie famous for its high levels of beta-carotene, and it's an inexpensive way to easily bump up your carbohydrate intake. When sliced into thin sticks and roasted with warm cinnamon and cumin, they transform into a delicious side dish worthy of any meal.

MAKES 2 SERVINGS

1 lb (454 g) carrots, washed and tops removed

1 tbsp (15 mL) avocado oil

½ tsp cinnamon

½ tsp ground cumin

¼ tsp sea salt

¼ tsp black pepper

Preheat the oven to 400°F/204°C and line a baking sheet with foil or parchment paper.

Cut the carrots into sticks by cutting each carrot in half vertically, then splitting each of those into quarters horizontally. Try to make the fries roughly the same size so they'll cook evenly.

Pile the carrot fries onto the baking sheet, drizzle with avocado oil and sprinkle with the spices and salt. Toss everything with your hands until the carrots are evenly coated.

Roast the carrots in the oven for 8 to 10 minutes or until they're lightly brown and crispy on the edges.

TOTAL RECIPE MACRONUTRIENTS (IN GRAMS PER SERVING)	
PROTEIN	2G
FAT	7G
TOTAL CARB	21G
NET CARB	15G

CURRIED LOTUS CHIPS

CRISPY, CRUNCHY AND SURPRISINGLY CARB-DENSE

One of my goals in this cookbook is to introduce you to some interesting and new sources of dietary carbohydrate that fit a Paleo template. Lotus is common in Asian cuisine, and when cooked, it tastes a lot like white potato. (If you're sensitive to nightshades that come from white potato, this may present an option for enjoying that familiar flavor without the consequences.) Half a cup (60 g) of lotus provides about 10 grams of carbohydrates. Here, I've sliced them thinly—I recommend a mandolin to ensure even cuts—fried them lightly in coconut oil and hit them with a shake of salt and hot curry powder. When it comes to seasoning options, let your imagination be your guide.

MAKES 2 SERVINGS

2 tsp (10 mL) lemon juice

¾ lb (340 g) lotus root

⅓ cup (78 mL) coconut oil

1 tsp sea salt

1 tsp hot curry powder

Fill a medium bowl with water and add the juice of half a lemon. Wash the lotus root. Using a mandolin or a very sharp knife, cut the lotus into ⅛-inch/3-millimeter slices. Add the slices to the lemon water and let them sit for at least 5 minutes. This is to prevent browning. Remove the lotus slices, and dry them on a paper towel.

Place a layer of paper towel onto a large plate, and get the salt and curry powder ready. Heat a large skillet—cast-iron is best—over medium heat, and add the coconut oil. Heat until the oil is very hot but not smoking. Working in batches, fry the lotus root in a single layer, about 3 to 4 minutes, or until they are crispy and brown on the edges. Remove them from the oil, and place them on the paper towel to drain. Immediately sprinkle them with sea salt and curry powder.

Eat fresh for crispiest results.

Look for lotus at Asian markets.

TOTAL RECIPE MACRONUTRIENTS (IN GRAMS PER SERVING)	
PROTEIN	4G
FAT	36G
TOTAL CARB	24G
NET CARB	17G

FIVE-MINUTE TORTILLAS

THE DO-IT-ALL WRAP THAT'LL REKINDLE YOUR LOVE OF BURRITOS

Handheld food is ultraconvenient for athletes, but once you're Paleo, flour and corn tortillas are off-limits because they contain inflammatory grains. Many of the gluten-free options I've tried fall apart and can't be wrapped or folded, so I went on a mission to make a sturdy version. These tortillas are soft, pliable and can withstand freezing and thawing. Get creative and make them into sweet or savory crepes, too!

MAKES 5 OR 6 (8"[20 CM]) TORTILLAS

4 large eggs

2 tsp (10 mL) melted ghee

2 tbsp (30 mL) water

½ cup (65 g) arrowroot or tapioca flour

2 tsp (6 g) coconut flour

Pinch of sea salt

Crack the eggs into a medium bowl, and whisk in the melted ghee and water. Add the dry ingredients—arrowroot, coconut flour and salt—and beat well to combine.

In a small (8-inch [20-centimeter]) ungreased nonstick skillet over medium heat, pour in about ¼ cup/59 milliliters of the batter, and immediately roll it around to evenly coat the bottom. The tortilla should start to pull away from the edges as it cooks. Cook for 1 minute on each side.

If saving for later, cool completely and store tightly wrapped or in an airtight glass container.

If making crepes for a sweet application, add ½ teaspoon vanilla.

TOTAL RECIPE MACRONUTRIENTS (IN GRAMS PER SERVING)	
PROTEIN	4G
FAT	5G
TOTAL CARB	10G
NET CARB	9G

PLANTAIN BISCUITS

SOMETIMES YOU JUST WANT A GLUTEN-FREE BISCUIT

I'm notoriously shy about Paleo baking, but this recipe materialized in my kitchen one day when I had a craving for Eggs Benedict. Not one for premade gluten-free breads, I stared at the green plantains on my counter and decided to experiment. The result is a biscuit with a dense texture, perfect for splitting open and dressing with poached eggs and a drizzle of ghee-based Hollandaise.

MAKES 6 SERVINGS

3 large eggs

2 green plantains, peeled and chopped

1 tbsp (15 mL) coconut oil

1 tsp baking powder

1 tbsp (7 g) almond meal

2 tsp (6 g) coconut flour

¾ tsp sea salt

Preheat the oven to 350°F/177°C, and line a baking sheet with parchment paper.

Combine all the ingredients in a high-powered blender or food processor. Blend everything together until you get a smooth, thick batter. Use a ¼-cup/59 millileters measuring cup to drop the batter onto the sheet. Bake for 12 to 15 minutes or until a knife inserted into the middle comes out clean.

Cool and eat!

Top with eggs and Hollandaise sauce for a Paleo version of Eggs Benedict.

TOTAL RECIPE MACRONUTRIENTS (IN GRAMS PER SERVING)	
PROTEIN	5G
FAT	5G
TOTAL CARB	20G
NET CARB	18G

OVEN-ROASTED SUNCHOKES

DELICATELY FLAVORED TUBERS ROASTED SIMPLY WITH GARLIC AND HERBS

There's probably a good chance you've never tried sunchokes. Also commonly known as Jerusalem artichokes, these little tubers—rootlike storage structures for a plant's energy—are rich in the carbohydrate inulin. Sunchokes somewhat resemble ginger and have thin, edible skin.

MAKES 4 SERVINGS

1 lb (454 g) sunchokes, washed and quartered

2 tsp (10 mL) avocado oil

2 cloves garlic, finely chopped

4 sprigs (1 g) thyme

½ tsp sea salt

¼ tsp black pepper

Preheat the oven to 400°F/204°C and line a baking sheet with foil or parchment paper. Place the sunchokes on the baking sheet, drizzle with avocado oil and sprinkle with garlic, thyme, salt and pepper. Toss everything with your hands until it's well-coated.

Roast the sunchokes for 15 to 20 minutes, or until they're tender when pierced with a fork and light brown around the edges. Stir once halfway through.

TOTAL RECIPE MACRONUTRIENTS (IN GRAMS PER SERVING)	
PROTEIN	3G
FAT	3G
TOTAL CARB	23G
NET CARB	20G

CREAMY COCONUT-BRAISED SWEET POTATOES

Cooking sweet potatoes can take forever, but recently I've started braising them to speed up the process. Braising is really a simple way of creating a golden brown crust, then adding a liquid and covering the pan until the food is cooked through. In the last few minutes, the cover is removed and the liquid is reduced, creating a really tasty sauce! Sweet potatoes are a delicious and affordable source of nutrient-dense carbohydrate.

MAKES 4 SERVINGS

1 tbsp (15 g) ghee

1 lb (454 g) orange sweet potatoes, peeled and cubed

1 cup (237 mL) coconut milk

2 tsp (6 g) cinnamon

1 tsp nutmeg

½ tsp sea salt

½ tsp pepper

Heat a large skillet or Dutch oven over medium-high heat, and warm the ghee until it melts and shimmers. Add the cubed sweet potatoes to the pan in a single layer. This is really important because if they're too crowded, they'll steam rather than brown and won't caramelize. Fry the sweet potatoes for about 2 minutes on each side until they develop a golden brown color on most sides. There's no need to be super precise.

Then pour in the coconut milk and add the cinnamon, nutmeg and salt. Bring the mixture just to a boil, then reduce the heat to low and simmer it, covered, for 10 to 15 minutes. Test the sweet potatoes for tenderness by piercing them with a fork.

Once they are cooked through, remove the lid and increase the heat to medium-high to reduce the coconut sauce, stirring often so the pieces don't stick. Once it's very thick, it's finished. Adjust the flavor with salt and pepper.

TOTAL RECIPE MACRONUTRIENTS (IN GRAMS PER SERVING)	
PROTEIN	3G
FAT	18G
TOTAL CARB	28G
NET CARB	23G

DUCK FAT ROASTED POTATOES WITH BLACK GARLIC

WHITE POTATOES ARE BACK ON THE MENU

For a long while, most Paleo folks avoided white potatoes for reasons they didn't quite understand—because that's just what the rules said. Turns out, if your blood sugar regulation and body composition are good, there's no good reason to keep them out of your diet, unless you are intolerant of nightshades. White potatoes, in fact, are a good source of glucose in addition to micronutrients such as potassium and Vitamin C. One thing you'll want to do is peel the potatoes, since antinutrients are prevalent in the skin. Black garlic has been fermented and has a sweet, mild flavor. If you can't find it, use half the amount of regular garlic instead.

MAKES 4 SERVINGS

2 lb (907 g) Yukon gold potatoes, peeled and diced

4 sprigs (1 g) fresh thyme, leaves removed

1 sprig (7 g) fresh rosemary, leaves removed and chopped

1 tsp sea salt

½ tsp black pepper

2 tbsp (30 mL) rendered duck fat, melted

4 cloves black garlic, finely chopped

Preheat the oven to 400°F/204°C and line a baking sheet with foil or parchment paper. Add the potatoes, thyme, rosemary, salt and pepper to the sheet, then drizzle everything with the melted duck fat. Toss well with your hands to coat the potatoes, then spread them out in a single layer. Roast the potatoes for about 45 to 50 minutes until they're golden brown. I stir them every 15 minutes so they brown evenly. Sprinkle with the black garlic in the last 10 minutes of roasting.

Substitute 2 cloves regular garlic for black garlic if you can't find it.

TOTAL RECIPE MACRONUTRIENTS (IN GRAMS PER SERVING)	
PROTEIN	6G
FAT	6G
TOTAL CARB	41G
NET CARB	38G

ROASTED SWEET POTATO SALAD
A DELICIOUS TAKE ON CLASSIC POTATO SALAD

Potato salad is one of those timeless side dishes that a lot of people give up when they start eating Paleo. With a few simple modifications, I'm upping nutrient-density and putting it back on the menu. Sweet potatoes provide good carbs for replenishing glycogen stores, and the chipotle mayo is loaded with healthy fats.

MAKES 4 SERVINGS

1 lb (454 g) orange sweet potatoes

3 green onions (2 oz [57 g]), white and light green parts, thinly sliced

3 tbsp (45 mL) Smoky Chipotle Mayo (page 209)

½ tsp sea salt

¼ tsp black pepper

3 strips cooked bacon, crumbled

3 tbsp (9 g) chopped fresh chives

Preheat the oven to 425°F/218°C and line a baking sheet with foil or parchment paper. Wash the sweet potatoes and put them on the baking sheet. Roast for about an hour or until a sharp knife easily pierces through the sweet potato. Remove them from the oven and allow them to cool. Then peel the skin off and cut the sweet potatoes into large cubes.

Add the roasted sweet potato, green onions, chipotle mayo, salt and pepper to a large bowl. Gently stir the mixture so the mayo evenly coats the potatoes but not hard enough to break up the pieces into mush. Sprinkle with crispy bacon and chives before serving.

Substitute white potatoes for sweet potatoes if needed.

TOTAL RECIPE MACRONUTRIENTS (IN GRAMS PER SERVING)	
PROTEIN	3G
FAT	12G
TOTAL CARB	21G
NET CARB	18G

GOLDEN BEET, FENNEL AND TOASTED HAZELNUT SALAD

A SATISFYING SIDE DISH FOR ANY MEAL

Beets are one of my favorite carb-dense veggies; when roasted, their natural sweetness really shines through. In this side dish, golden beets are roasted and paired with fresh fennel. The anise flavor of the fennel offsets the sweetness from the beets. I finish it off with toasted hazelnuts—one of the best nuts because of their low pro-inflammatory Omega-6 content—and a splash of oil and vinegar.

MAKES 4 SERVINGS

1 lb (454 g) golden beets, washed and tops trimmed off

1 tbsp (15 mL) avocado oil

¼ tsp sea salt

¼ tsp black pepper

¾ lb (340 g) fennel

¼ cup (37 g) unroasted hazelnuts

¼ red onion, very thinly sliced

1 tbsp (15 mL) balsamic vinegar

1 tbsp (15 mL) olive oil

Pinch of sea salt

Pinch of black pepper

Preheat the oven to 400°F/204°C and line a baking sheet with foil or parchment paper. Cut the beets into chunks about ¾ inch/19 millimeters thick. Place the beets on the baking sheet, drizzle with avocado oil and sprinkle with salt and pepper. Toss everything with your hands until it's well-coated. Roast the beets for 15 to 20 minutes, stirring once halfway through, or until they're tender when pierced with a fork. Remove from the oven and set aside to cool.

Meanwhile, prepare the rest of the salad. Trim the fronds off the fennel and set them aside for garnish. Quarter the fennel, cut the tough core out and discard it. Thinly slice the fennel. In a small dry skillet, toast the hazelnuts over medium heat, stirring often. Make sure to watch these because they can burn quite easily. This should take about 5 minutes.

To assemble the salad, arrange the roasted beets, fennel, red onion and hazelnuts in a single layer on a platter. Drizzle with the balsamic vinegar and olive oil, then sprinkle with a pinch of salt and pepper.

TOTAL RECIPE MACRONUTRIENTS (IN GRAMS PER SERVING)	
PROTEIN	4G
FAT	13G
TOTAL CARB	16G
NET CARB	10G

ROASTED BUTTERNUT CARROT SOUP

Soup is one of my favorite ways to sneak extra veggies into my daily routine, and this one is super tasty. Butternut squash is a darling of the fall and winter here in North America, and it's easy to find pre-peeled and cut to speed this preparation along. Butternut is loaded with Vitamins A and C, and per 100 grams has about 10 grams of net carbohydrates. When roasted and paired with carrots, ginger and turmeric, it's nutrient-dense and filling. Shredded chicken mixed in ups the protein content and makes it a full meal.

MAKES 4 TO 6 SERVINGS

2 lb (907 g) butternut squash, peeled, seeded and diced

1 lb (454 g) carrots, washed, tops removed and chopped

1 tbsp (15 mL) avocado oil

4 to 5 cups (946 to 1183 mL) chicken broth

1" (2.5 cm) piece ginger, peeled and sliced into coins

1" (2.5 cm) piece turmeric, peeled and chopped

¾ tsp sea salt

½ tsp black pepper

½ tsp garlic powder

½ tsp onion powder

Sea salt, to taste

Preheat the oven to 400°F/204°C and line two baking sheets with foil or parchment paper. Place the chopped butternut squash on one sheet and the chopped carrots onto the other, drizzling each sheet with half the oil and half the salt and pepper. Toss with your hands to combine evenly and spread the veggies out into an even layer. Roast the carrots for 25 to 30 minutes and the butternut squash for 30 to 40 minutes, stirring at least once during that time. Cool the veggies for 10 minutes.

Place the roasted butternut squash and carrots, 4 cups/946 milliliters of the chicken broth and the remaining ingredients into a high-powered blender or food processor. Blend until very smooth. You may have to do this in two batches depending on the size of your blender. If the soup is too thick, add more broth until it's as thin as you prefer. Adjust the amount of salt to taste.

This freezes well for about a month.

TOTAL RECIPE MACRONUTRIENTS (IN GRAMS PER SERVING)	
PROTEIN	6G
FAT	4G
TOTAL CARB	25G
NET CARB	20G

HASSELBACK SWEET POTATOES WITH COMPOUND HERB GHEE

DELICIOUSLY ROASTED SWEET POTATOES WITH A DOLLOP OF HEALTHY FAT

Hasselback potatoes originated in Sweden, and they make basic roasted spuds special. When roasted in the oven, the fan-shaped cuts get crispy and delicious. Top these sweet potatoes with a compound butter of ghee and fresh herbs for a sophisticated finish.

MAKES 2 TO 4 SERVINGS

1 lb (454 g) white sweet potatoes

1 tbsp (15 mL) melted ghee

1 tsp sea salt

2 tbsp (30 g) ghee

1 small clove garlic, finely chopped

1 tsp fresh chopped rosemary, about 1 sprig

1 tsp fresh thyme, about 5 sprigs

Preheat the oven to 400°F/204°C and line a baking sheet with foil or parchment paper. Scrub the skin of the sweet potatoes thoroughly. Use a very sharp knife to make several vertical cuts from the top of the sweet potatoes most of the way through, stopping about ¼ inch/6 millimeters from the bottom. Place the sweet potatoes on the baking sheet. Brush with the melted ghee and sprinkle the sea salt on top. Roast for 60 to 75 minutes, until the sweet potatoes are soft.

Meanwhile, make the compound ghee. In a small bowl, combine the ghee, garlic, rosemary and thyme. Stir well with a spoon until it forms a soft mixture. Top the hot roasted sweet potatoes with the compound ghee.

Use white potatoes instead of sweet potatoes. In this recipe, I make an exception about not eating the skin because it's so crispy.

TOTAL RECIPE MACRONUTRIENTS (IN GRAMS PER SERVING)	
PROTEIN	2G
FAT	10G
TOTAL CARB	21G
NET CARB	19G

CHINESE FIVE SPICE KABOCHA SQUASH

ROASTED SQUASH DUSTED WITH WARM SPICES

Chinese five spice is a spicy-sweet mixture of cinnamon, fennel, peppercorn, cloves and star anise. It's pretty easy to find in most markets, or if you're feeling adventurous, you can mix and grind your own. When sprinkled on kabocha squash and roasted, it makes a fantastic carb-dense side dish for virtually any meal. Kabocha is a green-skinned squash variety with dark orange flesh and a consistency similar to a sweet potato. Its shape makes it particularly tough to peel, but that's okay: The skin is thin and edible.

MAKES 4 TO 6 SERVINGS

2 lb (907 g) kabocha squash, halved and seeds removed

1 tbsp (15 mL) melted ghee

1 tsp Chinese five spice

½ tsp sea salt

¼ tsp ground ginger

Preheat the oven to 400°F/204°C and line two baking sheets with foil or parchment paper.

Place the kabocha squash halves, flat-side down, on a study cutting board. With a sharp knife, slice into ½-inch/13-millimeter semicircles. Divide the kabocha squash between the baking sheets, drizzling each with half the ghee and half the Chinese five spice, salt and ginger. Toss with your hands to combine evenly and spread the squash out into an even layer.

Roast the squash for about 45 minutes, flipping the slices once during cooking, until they're tender and golden brown around the edges.

Substitute butternut squash for kabocha.

TOTAL RECIPE MACRONUTRIENTS (IN GRAMS PER SERVING)	
PROTEIN	2G
FAT	3G
TOTAL CARB	6G
NET CARB	3G

ROASTED BEETS WITH ORANGE AND MINT

A SUPER-FRESH SIDE SALAD

There's something so fresh and classic about this combination of ingredients, and it's great served cold on a hot day. Save time by roasting the beets on your big cook-up day, then finish the salad off with the orange and mint when you're ready to eat!

MAKES 4 SERVINGS

4 lb (1814 g) red beets, tops trimmed off, diced into 1" (2.5 cm) pieces

2 tbsp (30 mL) avocado oil

1 tsp sea salt

2 oranges, cut into segments

Zest of 1 orange

4 tsp (20 mL) olive oil

2 tsp (10 mL) balsamic vinegar

¼ tsp sea salt

¼ tsp black pepper

⅓ cup (5 g) packed mint leaves, thinly sliced

Preheat the oven to 400°F/204°C and line a baking sheet with foil or parchment paper. Place the beets on the baking sheet, drizzle with avocado oil and sprinkle with salt. Toss everything with your hands until it's well-coated. Roast the beets for 45 to 60 minutes, stirring once halfway through, or until they're tender when pierced with a fork. Remove from the oven and set aside to cool.

On a serving plate, arrange the roasted beets with the oranges. In a small bowl, mix the orange zest, olive oil, balsamic vinegar, salt and pepper. Pour over the beets and oranges and garnish with mint leaves.

TOTAL RECIPE MACRONUTRIENTS (IN GRAMS PER SERVING)	
PROTEIN	6G
FAT	12G
TOTAL CARB	37G
NET CARB	27G

TWICE-BAKED STUFFED SWEET POTATOES

A NUTRIENT-DENSE TWIST ON AN OLD CLASSIC

Twice-baked potatoes are nothing new, but in this recipe, I've ramped up the nutrient density by adding kale and broccoli to the filling. Round out the flavor with garlic, shallots and some bacon for good measure, and you have a dish that'll satisfy even the pickiest vegetable eater. If you're feeling like white potatoes instead, those easily sub into this recipe, though you might have to adjust the initial baking time.

MAKES 4 SERVINGS

2 lb (454 g) yellow sweet potatoes

1 tbsp (15 g) ghee

1 medium shallot (2 oz [57 g]), chopped

2 cloves garlic, finely chopped

⅛ tsp + ¼ tsp sea salt

⅛ tsp + ¼ tsp black pepper

8 oz (227 g) broccoli crowns, chopped

1 medium bunch kale (10 oz [285 g]), tough stems removed, thinly sliced

4 slices cooked bacon, chopped

¼ tsp cayenne pepper

Smoky Chipotle Mayo (page 209), optional

Preheat the oven to 425°F/218°C and line a baking sheet with foil. Bake the potatoes, skin on, for 60 to 75 minutes or until fork tender. Remove from the oven and slice the cooked sweet potatoes in half lengthwise. Allow them to cool about 10 minutes or until you can comfortably handle them. Lower the oven temperature to 375°F/191°C.

Meanwhile, prepare the filling. In a large skillet over medium-low heat, add the ghee. Cook and stir the shallots, garlic, ⅛ teaspoon salt and ⅛ teaspoon pepper, about 4 minutes until softened but not brown. Add the broccoli and kale to the pan with ¼ teaspoon salt, ¼ teaspoon pepper and ¼ teaspoon cayenne pepper. Cook and stir about 5 minutes on medium or until the broccoli is cooked through. Turn off the heat and stir in the bacon.

Scoop out most of the flesh from the cooked sweet potato and put it into the pan with the other filling ingredients. Mix well until combined.

Time to fill the potatoes. Distribute the filling into the sweet potato shells, sprinkle with the bacon and then bake about 15 minutes at 375°F/191°C or until everything is heated through.

Serve with Smoky Chipotle Mayo on top.

TOTAL RECIPE MACRONUTRIENTS (IN GRAMS PER SERVING)	
PROTEIN	6G
FAT	7G
TOTAL CARB	44G
NET CARB	38G

CREAMY STEWED PLANTAINS

CARB-RICH COMFORT FOOD

Plantains are such a great source of Paleo-friendly carbohydrates. When green, they're hard and starchy, like a potato. When black, they're soft and are great for sweet preparations. In this dish, yellow plantains with some black markings are perfect because they're mildly sweet, but won't fall apart to mush when cooked.

MAKES 4 SERVINGS

1 tbsp (15 mL) coconut oil

1 medium onion (10 oz [284 g]), diced

1 red bell pepper (8 oz [227 g]), diced

1 tsp sea salt

2 bay leaves

3 cloves garlic, finely chopped

¼ cup (59 mL) chicken broth

4 medium ripe (yellow) plantains, peeled and cut into ½" (13 mm) pieces

1 can (14 oz [414 mL]) full-fat coconut milk

½ cup (116 g) diced tomatoes

Heat a large high-sided skillet or a Dutch oven over medium heat and add the coconut oil. Cook and stir the onion, red pepper and salt for about 10 minutes or until softened and lightly brown. Add the bay leaves and garlic. Cook and stir for 30 seconds, until the garlic is fragrant. Add the chicken broth to deglaze the pan, scraping up any brown bits from the bottom. Then add the plantains, coconut milk and tomatoes. Bring the mixture to a boil then reduce to a simmer. Cook, covered, for about 10 minutes. Then remove the cover and continue simmering another 3 to 4 minutes, until the coconut milk has thickened.

This dish is also great served over cauliflower rice or white rice.

TOTAL RECIPE MACRONUTRIENTS (IN GRAMS PER SERVING)	
PROTEIN	5G
FAT	19G
TOTAL CARB	67G
NET CARB	60G

SAVORY MUSHROOM TAPIOCA

IT'S NOT JUST FOR DESSERT!

Tapioca is widely known for its power as a gluten-free thickener and is most popular in sweet recipes such as tapioca pudding. I'm turning the tables here as a savory preparation! Tapioca—derived from the manioc/cassava root—is dense in starchy carbohydrates and thickens when cooked. Dried mushrooms, chicken broth and fresh herbs add flavor to what otherwise is a blank canvas.

MAKES 4 SERVINGS

1 cup (237 mL) + 1 cup (237 mL) water

½ cup (90 g) small tapioca pearls

1 oz (28 g) dried shiitake mushrooms

½ oz (14 g) dried porcini mushrooms

2 cups (473 mL) chicken broth

2 tbsp (30 g) ghee

¼ tsp black pepper

1 tsp fresh thyme

¼ cup (2 oz [57g]) chopped fresh parsley

Sea salt, to taste

Soak the tapioca pearls in 1 cup/237 milliliters cold water for about 20 minutes. Meanwhile, boil the other cup/237 milliliters of water and put the dried mushrooms in a heat-resistant bowl. Pour the boiling water onto the mushrooms and allow them to rehydrate for about 10 minutes or until they're soft. Drain the water and put the mushrooms aside. When the tapioca is done soaking, drain the water.

Put the soaked tapioca, chicken broth, ghee and pepper in a medium pot. Bring the mixture to a boil, then reduce to a simmer. Cook this on low for about 8 minutes or until the tapioca is soft and the liquid is absorbed. Stir in the rehydrated mushrooms, thyme and parsley. Add salt to taste, if needed.

TOTAL RECIPE MACRONUTRIENTS (IN GRAMS PER SERVING)	
PROTEIN	4G
FAT	8G
TOTAL CARB	26G
NET CARB	24G

TARO PUREE

ADD A CARB PUNCH TO ANY SHAKE

The first time I tasted taro was in Hawaii when it was mixed into a tropical fruit shake. I was blown away. The taro puree was so neutral in flavor that I couldn't taste it, yet it made the shake creamy and satisfying. I knew I had to replicate the method so I could add it to post-workout protein shakes for added starchy carbs. This taro puree is the base recipe that I use for those post-workout shakes. I make a batch then freeze it into ice cube trays for easy use later on.

MAKES 4 CUPS (474 ML)

2 lb (907 g) taro root, peeled and diced

½ to ¾ cup (118 to 177 mL) water

Place the peeled and diced taro into a large pot and add water until the taro is submerged completely. Bring to a boil, then reduce to a simmer. Cook for approximately 10 minutes or until the taro is fork tender. Drain and cool.

Add about half the taro to a food processor or blender with 2 to 3 ounces/60 to 89 milliliters water. Blend the taro until it's a smooth puree. If it looks too thick, keep adding water 1 tablespoon/15 milliliters at a time. It should be about the consistency of applesauce. Repeat this with the other half of the taro.

Scoop the puree into 2 ice cube trays and freeze until solid, then store in a plastic zip-top bag.

Drop 2 cubes into a post-workout shake for a carb boost.

TOTAL RECIPE MACRONUTRIENTS (IN GRAMS PER SERVING)	
PROTEIN	7G
FAT	0G
TOTAL CARB	268G
NET CARB	220G

CARROT PARSNIP FRITTERS

FRITTERS: NOT JUST FOR POTATOES ANYMORE

Parsnips and carrots are two really flavorful carb-dense root veggies, and they play quite nicely off one another. When shredded and salted, the excess moisture is drawn out, then squeezed away. This technique allows the fritters to stick together without generating too much steam inside and falling apart.

MAKES 6 SERVINGS

2 medium parsnips (12 oz [340 g]), shredded

2 small carrots (3 oz [85 g]), shredded

½ tsp sea salt

3 large eggs, beaten

1 tsp dried dill

2 tsp (6 g) dried onion flakes

½ tsp dried thyme

¼ tsp black pepper

¼ tsp red pepper flakes

1 tbsp (15 mL) coconut oil

Garlic Aioli (page 206), optional

Combine the parsnips, carrots and salt in a large bowl, and let everything sit for 10 to 15 minutes. Using your hands, squeeze the moisture out of the parsnips and carrots. Wringing it out between a few layers of cheesecloth gives the best results. Add the beaten eggs, dill, onion flakes, thyme and peppers to the mixture and stir to combine everything.

Heat a large skillet over medium heat and add the coconut oil. Drop the mixture by the rounded tablespoon into the pan, and flatten it out slightly with a spatula. Don't crowd the pan. Cook for 3 to 4 minutes per side or until the fritter is lightly browned. Cool these on a baking rack so the bottoms don't get soggy. Repeat this process until the fritter mixture is used up.

Serve with a dollop of Garlic Aioli.

TOTAL RECIPE MACRONUTRIENTS (IN GRAMS PER SERVING)	
PROTEIN	4G
FAT	5G
TOTAL CARB	17G
NET CARB	12G

CHAPTER FIVE

NUTRIENT-BOOSTING VEGGIE SIDES

It's time to really embrace veggies for what they are: Powerhouses that provide crucial micronutrients, meant to be consumed daily. Somewhere along the way, Paleo has adopted a reputation for being all meat and fat, but that couldn't be further from the truth.

Veggies, both raw and cooked in a variety of colors, are the superstars of every balanced main meal. When it comes to fruit, eat less than you do veggies, but it's certainly fine to add them to your plate once or twice a day. An oft-forgotten way to prepare and eat veggies is in their fermented state. Easy to find and already prepared, options such as sauerkraut and kimchi provide a dose of beneficial probiotic bacteria that helps keep the gut in tip-top form.

It's best to eat as many different vegetables as possible to get an array of vitamins, minerals and antioxidants in your diet. Buy the best quality your budget allows, and when possible enjoy the fruit and veggies that are freshest and in season where you live.

SUMMER SALAD WITH SALT AND PEPPER SHRIMP

This salad is bursting with bold summer flavors, and it's best to make when the ingredients are fresh and in season. Sweet watermelon and bold cherry tomatoes are complemented by cool avocado and fragrant basil, and they're tossed in a tangy, lemony dressing. If you're serving a crowd, this recipe easily doubles, and it's just as delicious without the shrimp.

MAKES 4 SERVINGS

2 cups (340 g) diced watermelon

1 cup (170 g) cherry tomatoes, halved

2 medium avocados (10 oz [284 g]), pitted and diced

¼ cup (20 g) basil leaves

Tangy Lemon Dressing (page xx)

1 lb (454 g) large shrimp, peeled and deveined

¼ tsp sea salt

¼ tsp black pepper

1 tbsp (15 mL) coconut oil or ghee

In a large bowl, mix the watermelon, tomatoes, avocado, basil and Tangy Lemon Dressing. Stir to coat the salad with the dressing.

Pat the shrimp dry with a paper towel and sprinkle them with salt and pepper. Toss to make sure they're very well-coated. Heat a large skillet over medium-high heat, then add the coconut oil. Place the shrimp in the skillet in one single layer and cook for 1 minute on each side or until they're no longer translucent and are light golden brown.

Serve the salad on plates with the shrimp arranged on top.

This dish pairs well with grilled chicken.

TOTAL RECIPE MACRONUTRIENTS (IN GRAMS PER SERVING)	
PROTEIN	26G
FAT	28G
TOTAL CARB	17G
NET CARB	10G

HERBED OLIVES

OLIVES, TAKEN UP A NOTCH

It's easy to forget that the humble olive is a fantastic source of healthy dietary fats, particularly those of the monounsaturated variety. Here I've added a complement of flavors such as orange, fennel and thyme to elevate these olives from plain to special. My favorite olive variety for this recipe is called Castelvetrano and hails from Sicily. It has a mild, buttery flavor and an unmistakable vivid green flesh.

MAKES 4 SERVINGS

½ lb (227 g) green olives

Zest of 1 small orange

1 tbsp (15 mL) orange juice

1 tbsp (15 mL) olive oil

1 tsp fennel seeds

½ tsp fresh thyme

¼ tsp red pepper flakes

Combine all the ingredients in a small bowl and mix well. For best results, let the flavors mingle for at least 30 minutes before serving.

TOTAL RECIPE MACRONUTRIENTS (IN GRAMS PER SERVING)	
PROTEIN	1G
FAT	9G
TOTAL CARB	5G
NET CARB	3G

CRUNCHY SLAW WITH CHICKEN

NUTRIENT-RICH SLAW THAT PACKS A PROTEIN PUNCH, A HINT OF SWEET AND A LITTLE HEAT

Crisp, fresh veggies are the star of this dish, and the flavors are big and bold. Green cabbage, a cruciferous vegetable, is a rich source of vitamins and minerals. It's a powerhouse! The snap peas, while technically in the bean family, are tender and green. Because they can be eaten raw and are mostly fleshy pod, they fit the Paleo template. Top this slaw off with some cashews for healthy fat, and you have a complete meal.

MAKES 4 SERVINGS

1 lb (454 g) cabbage, cored and thinly sliced

½ medium bell pepper (4 oz [114 g]), any color, thinly sliced

2 stalks (4 oz [114 g]) celery, thinly sliced

4 oz (114 g) sugar snap peas, tough stems removed and halved

3 green onions (2 oz [57 g]), white and light green parts, thinly sliced

¼ cup (9 g) cilantro leaves, packed

1 lb (454 g) cooked chicken breasts, shredded

Creamy Mango Jalapeño Dressing (page 212)

½ tsp sea salt

¼ tsp black pepper

¼ cup (35 g) unroasted cashews, roughly chopped

Combine the cabbage, bell pepper, celery, sugar snap peas, green onions and cilantro in a very large bowl and toss to combine. Add the shredded chicken breast and dressing, stirring until everything is well-coated. Adjust the seasoning with salt and pepper, and garnish with the cashews.

Omit the chicken for a veggie-only side dish.

TOTAL RECIPE MACRONUTRIENTS (IN GRAMS PER SERVING)	
PROTEIN	24G
FAT	20G
TOTAL CARB	25G
NET CARB	19G

CIDER-BRAISED CABBAGE, APPLE AND ONION

CARAMELIZED VEGGIES WITH A TOUCH OF SWEETNESS

Cabbage is an incredibly nutrient-dense, yet inexpensive, cruciferous veggie. It's well known for its pungent sulfur compounds, but when sautéed with sweet apple and onion, then braised with a bit of hard cider, it becomes incredibly tender and mild. By caramelizing the veggies first, you'll develop lots of delicious flavor. The alcohol in the hard cider cooks off. Serve a hearty portion alongside succulent pulled pork for a new version of this classic pairing.

MAKES 4 SERVINGS

1 medium green cabbage

1 tbsp (15 g) ghee

½ large white onion, thinly sliced

1 red apple, thinly sliced

¾ tsp sea salt

½ tsp black pepper

1 cup (237 mL) hard cider

Prepare the cabbage by removing the tough outer leaves and slicing it in half from top to bottom. Then cut the cabbage into 4 to 6 wedges per half. You want them thin enough that they'll cook through quickly but not so thin that they disintegrate.

Heat a very large skillet or Dutch oven over medium heat and add the ghee, onion, apple, salt and pepper to the skillet. Cook and stir for about 5 minutes or until everything starts to soften and gets golden brown. Now nestle the cabbage wedges in the pan and cook for about 5 minutes so they can develop some color. Flip the cabbage and cook for 5 more minutes. Add the cider and bring the liquid to a boil. Then cover the skillet or Dutch oven and reduce the heat to a simmer.

Simmer the veggies for about 15 minutes. Then uncover the skillet and turn the heat to medium-high so the cider reduces to a thick sauce that coats the veggies, about 8 minutes.

If you don't want to use hard cider, substitute chicken broth.

TOTAL RECIPE MACRONUTRIENTS (IN GRAMS PER SERVING)	
PROTEIN	1G
FAT	4G
TOTAL CARB	15G
NET CARB	13G

CARAMELIZED BRUSSELS SPROUTS WITH SUN-DRIED TOMATOES AND PINE NUTS

TINY BUT PACKED WITH FLAVOR

Brussels sprouts have a bad rep for being dense miniature cabbages, but when caramelized and tossed with garlic, sundried tomatoes and pine nuts, they're so delicious. The secret is to steam them through, then crisp up the edges in a cast-iron skillet. Brussels sprouts, another cruciferous veggie, are packed with micronutrients.

MAKES 4 SERVINGS

1 lb (454 g) Brussels sprouts, halved

2 tbsp (30 mL) avocado oil

¾ cup (80 g) sun-dried tomatoes, sliced

4 cloves garlic, finely chopped

¼ cup (36 g) pine nuts

½ tsp sea salt

¼ tsp black pepper

In a medium pot, steam the halved Brussels sprouts in a steamer basket over water for about 10 minutes or until fork tender. Set aside.

Heat a large skillet over medium-high heat and add the avocado oil. Stir and cook the Brussels sprouts until they start to brown on the edges, about 8 minutes. Then add the sun-dried tomatoes, garlic, pine nuts, salt and pepper. Cook and stir another minute, until the garlic is fragrant and the nuts are lightly toasted.

TOTAL RECIPE MACRONUTRIENTS (IN GRAMS PER SERVING)

PROTEIN	8G
FAT	11G
TOTAL CARB	22G
NET CARB	15G

ROASTED PLUM TOMATOES WITH PANCETTA

THE HUMBLE TOMATO GETS

Roasting tomatoes in the oven concentrates their
these in the oven on my weekly cook-up day and s
of cured Italian pork—adds a salty, savory counte
prosciutto instead.

MAKES 4 SERVINGS

1 ½ lb (680 g) plum tomatoes, halved and
seeded

1 tbsp (15 mL) avocado oil

2 tsp (10 mL) balsamic vinegar

1 tsp sea salt

½ tsp black pepper

½ tsp dried Italian herbs

¼ lb (113 g) thinly sliced pancetta

Fresh basil leaves for garnish, optional

Preheat the oven to 325°F/163°C and line a baking sheet with foil or parchment paper.

Arrange the halved and seeded plum tomatoes in a single layer. Drizzle the tomatoes with avocado oil and vinegar, then sprinkle with sea salt, black pepper and Italian herbs. Bake for 90 minutes or until the tomatoes have softened and begin to caramelize on the edges.

Right before serving, top each tomato half with a small piece of pancetta and garnish with basil, if desired.

TOTAL RECIPE MACRONUTRIENTS (IN GRAMS PER SERVING)

PROTEIN	9G
FAT	6G
TOTAL CARB	8G
NET CARB	7G

STRAWBERRY COCONUT KALE SALAD

Kale is widely renowned as one of the most nutrient-dense vegetables, but when eaten raw, it has a reputation for being bitter and tough. By massaging the kale with olive oil, salt and pepper, you'll break it down and soften the texture. To balance the bitterness, fresh strawberries, coconut and balsamic add a sweet finish.

MAKES 4 SERVINGS

½ lb (227 g) bunch of kale, tough lower stems removed and thinly sliced

1 tbsp (15 mL) olive oil

⅛ tsp sea salt

⅛ tsp black pepper

½ lb (227 g) strawberries, stems removed and sliced

3 tbsp (45 mL) balsamic vinegar

⅓ cup (27 g) unsweetened coconut flakes

¼ tsp pink peppercorns, crushed with the back of a knife, optional

Place the kale, olive oil, salt and pepper in a large bowl. Using your hands, massage the kale by scrunching the leaves; this softens the kale and makes it less tough. For best results, let the massaged kale sit for 30 minutes before making the rest of the salad.

Add the strawberries, vinegar, coconut flakes and pink peppercorns. Mix the salad well, then adjust the seasonings with salt and pepper.

TOTAL RECIPE MACRONUTRIENTS (IN GRAMS PER SERVING)

PROTEIN	2G
FAT	6G
TOTAL CARB	11G
NET CARB	8G

SWISS CHARD SALAD WITH TOASTED WALNUTS

TOASTY WALNUTS, LEMON AND HERBS ADD FLAVOR TO THIS HUMBLE GREEN

Chard is such a versatile leafy green, and it's great served both raw and cooked. It's particularly rich in vitamin A and lots of antioxidants. The warm walnut dressing wilts the chard just a bit when you pour it over the greens. If you're going to prep the salad ahead of time, warm the dressing back up before you add it to the chard.

MAKES 4 SERVINGS

1 medium shallot (2 oz [57 g]), finely chopped

1 clove garlic, finely chopped

1 tsp chopped fresh rosemary

2 tbsp (30 mL) avocado oil

1 tsp sea salt

½ tsp black pepper

1 ½ cups (170 g) walnut halves

1 medium bunch Swiss chard (9 oz [255 g]), sliced

1 tbsp (15 mL) lemon juice

1 tbsp (15 mL) apple cider vinegar

In a medium skillet over low heat, combine the shallot, garlic, rosemary, avocado oil, salt and pepper. Cook and stir, about 3 minutes, until the shallots turn translucent and soften. Add the nuts, cooking and stirring on low heat until they're evenly toasted and lightly browned. Turn off the heat.

In a large bowl, combine the Swiss chard with the lemon juice and vinegar. Pour the walnut mixture over the chard and toss well to combine.

TOTAL RECIPE MACRONUTRIENTS (IN GRAMS PER SERVING)	
PROTEIN	11G
FAT	31G
TOTAL CARB	7G
NET CARB	5G

TAJÍN SALAD

Back in 2007 when I was racing downhill mountain bikes, I traveled to Ensenada in Baja, California, for an event. Pista Escalones was a dusty, fun track, and I luckily made it down in one piece. After the race, I bought fresh fruit with lime juice and Tajín (pronounced ta-heen)—a Mexican seasoning of lime, salt and chili pepper—from a vendor near the finish line. The combination of sweet, salty and a little spicy was hard to forget! I've been making this Tajín-inspired salad as a fantastic partner to grilled chicken or fish on warm summer evenings. I use thin-skinned cucumbers such as Persian or English varieties because they don't need to be peeled.

MAKES 6 SERVINGS

2 cups (5 oz [284 g]) diced watermelon

1 cup (150 g) diced jicama

1 cup (142 g) diced cucumber

2 medium avocados (10 oz [284 g]), pitted and diced

Zest of 2 limes

2 tbsp (30 mL) lime juice

1 tsp ground ancho chili pepper

¼ tsp ground chipotle pepper

½ tsp sea salt

Place all the ingredients in a large bowl, and stir to combine.

Add diced mango or pineapple to change it up.

TOTAL RECIPE MACRONUTRIENTS (IN GRAMS PER SERVING)	
PROTEIN	1G
FAT	6G
TOTAL CARB	8G
NET CARB	5G

GADO GADO WITH SPICY SATAY SAUCE

THE PERFECT PARTY OR PICNIC DISH

I had Gado Gado for the first time when I traveled to Indonesia in 2011. On the island of Bali, Gado Gado is served on big plates at roadside *warungs* (cafes) as a casual lunch or snack. The exact ingredients vary a bit, but there was always a mix of fresh and steamed veggies with some sort of protein, like tofu. Since soy isn't part of a Paleo template, I replaced it with shrimp, but you could easily do other proteins such as diced chicken. The satay sauce uses tahini—sesame paste—instead of peanuts to re-create the flavor of that traditional sweet-spicy topping.

MAKES 6 SERVINGS

FOR THE GADO GADO

¼ lb (113 g) cauliflower florets

¼ lb (113 g) green beans, trimmed and chopped in half

1 lb (454 g) shrimp, peeled and deveined

½ lb (227 g) cucumber, peeled and sliced into rounds

¼ lb (113 g) cherry tomatoes, halved

4 hard-cooked eggs, peeled and halved

FOR THE SPICY SATAY SAUCE

1 red jalapeño pepper

¼ cup (59 mL) tahini

¼ cup (59 mL) water

5 garlic cloves

1 tbsp (15 mL) raw honey

1 tsp coconut aminos

1 tsp fish sauce

¼ tsp sea salt

1 tbsp (9 g) chopped cashews, garnish

Start by steaming the veggies. Place the cauliflower in a medium pot fitted with a steamer basket and fill the bottom of the pot with about 1 inch/2.5 centimeters of water. Put the cover on and bring the water to a boil. Steam the cauliflower for 3 to 4 minutes, then add the green beans and steam another 2 to 3 minutes. Remove to a bowl, and let these cool.

Next steam the shrimp. In the same pot and steamer basket, steam the shrimp for about 2 minutes or until they turn pink. Let these cool before serving.

Arrange the platter with the steamed veggies, fresh veggies, shrimp and eggs.

To make the satay sauce, place all the ingredients in a high-powered blender or food processor and blend until smooth. Pour the sauce into a small pot and bring to a boil, then reduce to a simmer for 5 minutes. Let it cool, then serve it in a small bowl on the platter for dipping. Top the satay sauce with the chopped cashews.

Add steamed baby potatoes to bump up the carb content.

TOTAL RECIPE MACRONUTRIENTS (IN GRAMS PER SERVING)	
PROTEIN	23G
FAT	11G
TOTAL CARB	12G
NET CARB	9G

SAVORY CAULIFLOWER RICE

THE SIDE DISH THAT GOES WITH VIRTUALLY EVERYTHING

Cauliflower "rice" is a staple you can use as a base or side dish for a plethora of recipes. When cut into small enough pieces, the cauliflower resembles grains of rice and has a neutral flavor to build on. In fact, you'll find this recipe pairs with others in the book, including Korean Bibimbap (page 98) and the Badass Bowl (page 97). Once you're comfortable with the basic method, start playing around with different flavor profiles to match any cuisine.

MAKES 4 SERVINGS

1 ½ lb (680 g) cauliflower, cored

1 tbsp (15 mL) coconut oil

3 cloves garlic, finely chopped

1 tbsp (15 mL) coconut aminos

½" (13 mm) piece ginger, peeled and minced

½ tsp sea salt

¼ tsp black pepper

The best way to rice cauliflower is in a food processor fitted with a shredding or grating blade. Another option is to use a regular blade by adding the cauliflower in a few batches and pulsing it until small pieces the size of rice form.

Heat a large skillet over medium heat, then add the coconut oil and minced garlic. Cook and stir for about 30 seconds, until the garlic is fragrant. Turn up the heat to high and add the cauliflower, stirring so the pieces don't stick to the bottom of the skillet. Stir in the coconut aminos, ginger, salt and pepper. Continue to cook and stir for 6 to 8 minutes or until the cauliflower is tender but not mushy.

TOTAL RECIPE MACRONUTRIENTS (IN GRAMS PER SERVING)

PROTEIN	4G
FAT	4G
TOTAL CARB	11G
NET CARB	6G

ZUCCHINI NOODLES WITH ARUGULA, BACON AND BURST CHERRY TOMA[...]

A SURPRISINGLY SIMPLE AND FRESH SIDE DISH FOR ANY M[...]

Zucchini noodles—or zoodles, as they're affectionately called—are incredibly versatile in Paleo cooking. The key to [...] perfect texture is to salt the zucchini after you've julienned or spiral-cut it; that'll wick out some of the moisture, keepi[...] your noodles from getting waterlogged. Arugula adds a peppery note to balance out the sweetness from the cherry tomatoes. This green is high in vitamin A and is one of the richest vegetable sources of vitamin K.

MAKES 2 SERVINGS

3 medium zucchini (24 oz [680g])

1 tsp sea salt

1 ½ cups (250 g) cherry tomatoes

1 tbsp (15 mL) olive oil

2 cloves garlic, finely chopped

1 cup (35 g) packed arugula

¼ tsp sea salt

¼ tsp black pepper

⅛ tsp red pepper flakes

4 slices crispy cooked bacon, chopped

First, prep the zucchini noodles. Use a julienne peeler—my favorite method because the peelers are inexpensive and make a thin "noodle"—or a spiral slicer. Place the zucchini noodles in a colander or strainer and sprinkle them with the salt. Toss the zucchini with the salt and allow it to drain over a bowl or into the sink for at least 15 minutes. Rinse the noodles well with water and squeeze them gently to drain as much of the moisture as possible. Set aside.

Next get the cherry tomatoes going. In a large skillet over medium heat, add the olive oil and cherry tomatoes. Cook these for about 10 minutes until the tomatoes soften and burst open. Hint: You may want to cover these partially with a lid so they don't splatter. Add the garlic, stirring and cooking until it's fragrant, about 30 seconds. Then add the zucchini noodles, and cook for another 2 minutes until they're heated through. Turn off the heat and stir in the arugula until it's wilted. Season with additional salt, if needed, and the pepper.

Plate the zucchini noodles and sprinkle with the chopped bacon.

TOTAL RECIPE MACRONUTRIENTS (IN GRAMS PER SERVING)

PROTEIN	9G
FAT	14G
TOTAL CARB	17G
NET CARB	12G

COMFORTING CREAMY BROCCOLI SOUP

Creamy, milk-based soups are usually off the menu if you're avoiding dairy, but this recipe will change all that. Coconut milk is paired with chicken broth and aromatics to create the base, then it's simmered with broccoli and pureed to make a creamy soup that you'll love. Sometimes I top this with roasted chicken for a complete meal.

MAKES 3 TO 4 SERVINGS

1 large leek (8 oz [227 g]), white and light green parts, washed and sliced

½ small white onion (2 oz [57 g]), chopped

1 lb (454 g) broccoli crowns, chopped

4 cups (946 mL) chicken broth

1 cup (237 mL) full-fat coconut milk

1 tbsp (15 g) ghee

2 cloves garlic, chopped

½ tsp sea salt

¼ tsp black pepper

Add all the ingredients to a large pot and bring them to a boil. Reduce to a simmer, uncovered, for about 30 minutes. Carefully transfer the soup to a blender and puree until smooth. Adjust the seasoning with salt and pepper to taste.

Substitute cauliflower for broccoli.

TOTAL RECIPE MACRONUTRIENTS (IN GRAMS PER SERVING)	
PROTEIN	9G
FAT	20G
TOTAL CARB	13G
NET CARB	9G

CHAPTER SIX

TASTY & NUTRITIOUS

TREATS

Sometimes you want a little something sweet and these treats pack a nutritious punch. Instead of Paleo cakes, cookies and baked goods, I'll whip up one of these treats to satisfy a craving because they're less likely to put my sweet tooth into overdrive.

Many of these tasty treats are fortified with goodies like high-quality gelatin, extra protein and fast-burning fats so you get more nutritional benefit from the indulgence. Plus, limiting the use of low-nutrient value sugars and using fruit as the primary sweetener make these better choices. I try to keep my indulgences to once a week so they stay a special treat.

SAVORY SALT AND VINEGAR COCONUT CHIPS

ONCE YOU START SNACKING ON THESE, IT'LL BE HARD TO STOP!

There's something about this snack that's pretty addictive. I took the flavors of traditional salt and vinegar chips and made these crispy baked coconut chips instead. Coconut is packed with healthy saturated fats and the coconut vinegar gives it a bit of tang.

MAKES 8 SERVINGS

2 cups (100 g) unsweetened coconut flakes

2 tbsp (30 mL) coconut vinegar

½ tsp honey

½ tsp sea salt

Preheat the oven to 350°F/177°C and line a baking sheet with foil or parchment paper.

In a medium bowl, combine the coconut flakes, coconut vinegar, honey and salt. Mix the ingredients really well, until the coconut flakes are evenly coated.

Spread the coconut flakes in an even layer on the baking sheet, and bake until crispy and golden, about 8 minutes. Stir the coconut flakes about halfway through. Cool and store in an airtight container.

Make a chipotle lime flavor by using 2 cups/100 grams unsweetened coconut flakes, zest of 1 lime, 2 tablespoons/30 milliliters lime juice, ½ teaspoon ground chipotle pepper and ½ teaspoon sea salt. Follow the same above directions.

TOTAL RECIPE MACRONUTRIENTS (IN GRAMS PER SERVING)	
PROTEIN	1G
FAT	7G
TOTAL CARB	4G
NET CARB	2G

RASPBERRY LIME GUMMIES

JOINT-SOOTHING GELATIN IN A SWEET-TART BITE

These gummies are the perfect blend of sweet raspberries and tart lime, along with good-for-you gelatin. Training puts a burden on your body, and gelatin has been shown to have soothing properties for sore joints. Bonus: It's also great for gut health. And while natural sources of gelatin, such as bone broth, are great, sometimes it's easier to eat in these naturally flavored bite-size gummies.

MAKES 12 SERVINGS

1 tsp (15 mL) coconut oil

2 cups (260 g) raspberries

1 cup (237 mL) unsweetened coconut water

Zest of 2 limes

1 tbsp (15 mL) lime juice

1 tbsp (15 mL) raw honey

3 tbsp (21 g) high-quality grass-fed gelatin

Grease an 8-inch x 8-inch/20-centimeter x 20-centimeter glass dish with coconut oil and set aside.

In a blender or food processor, puree the raspberries and coconut water. Put the mixture through a fine mesh strainer to remove the seeds and collect the juice in a medium saucepan.

Add the lime zest, lime juice and honey to the juice and stir to combine. Gently warm the mixture over low heat. You only want to warm it enough to dissolve the gelatin, so don't allow it to boil. Once the juice is warm, begin to whisk in the gelatin 1 tablespoon/7 grams at a time.

Turn off the heat and pour the mixture into the greased dish. Refrigerate until set, usually 1 to 2 hours. Store tightly wrapped in the refrigerator and consume within 1 to 3 days. The gummies will lose water the longer they sit, making them chewier.

You can substitute strawberries for the raspberries.

TOTAL RECIPE MACRONUTRIENTS (IN GRAMS PER SERVING)	
PROTEIN	1G
FAT	1G
TOTAL CARB	9G
NET CARB	7G

MOCHA PROTEIN ALMOND BUTTER

ALMOND BUTTER, ELEVATED.

Homemade almond butter is cost-effective and a great source of healthy fats, but the plain stuff can be a bit boring. I added cocoa and coffee for a deep mocha flavor, and adding a scoop of your favorite protein bumps up the amino acid content. If you can find almonds without the skins, use those; the almond butter will taste better. I look for slivered almonds in the bulk bin section of my local market!

MAKES 10 SERVINGS

1 cup (130 g) slivered almonds

2 tbsp (14 g) cocoa powder

2 tbsp (12 g) protein powder, optional

1 tbsp (15 mL) coconut oil, melted

1 tbsp (15 mL) raw honey

1 heaping tsp ground coffee

¼ tsp sea salt

Preheat the oven to 350°F/177°C and line a large baking sheet with foil or parchment paper. Spread the slivered almonds in a single layer on the sheet and bake for about 8 minutes, until the almonds are golden brown. It's a good idea to stir them halfway through so they brown evenly.

In a high-powered blender or food processor, combine the roasted slivered almonds, cocoa, protein powder, honey, coconut oil, coffee and salt. Process on high until the nuts are broken down and everything is smooth. You may need to stop the blender and scrape down the sides a couple of times to get all the nuts incorporated.

Store in an airtight container in the refrigerator.

TOTAL RECIPE MACRONUTRIENTS (IN GRAMS PER SERVING)	
PROTEIN	4G
FAT	9G
TOTAL CARB	6G
NET CARB	4G

ALMOND BUTTER AND JELLY BITES

Growing up, peanut butter and jelly sandwiches were a common lunch for us kids because, let's face it, the flavor combination is classic. While peanuts are not part of a Paleo template, almonds are a great substitute. In this recipe, dried apricots act as the jelly paired with almonds and salted almond butter. The result is a lightly sweet treat perfect for individual popping.

MAKES ABOUT 24 BITES

½ cup (250 g) unroasted almonds

½ cup (20 g) unsweetened coconut flakes

½ lb (227 g) Medjool dates, pitted

1 cup (170 g) dried apricots, chopped

¼ cup (64 g) salted almond butter

½ tsp sea salt

Place the almonds and coconut flakes in a food processor and pulse long enough until the nuts are broken down and chunky. Some pieces will be small and some will be bigger, but you don't want to make almond butter out of it! Add the dates, apricots, almond butter and salt, and process until the mixture resembles coarse crumbs.

Use about 1 large spoonful of the mixture and roll it into a ball. Repeat until all the mixture is used up.

TOTAL RECIPE MACRONUTRIENTS (IN GRAMS PER SERVING)	
PROTEIN	3G
FAT	7G
TOTAL CARB	14G
NET CARB	11G

PISTACHIO LEMON COCONUT BITES

A SWEET BITE WITH A POP OF PROTEIN

I've taken the ubiquitous date-based fruit and nut bar, added some lemon for a fresh flavor and sprinkled in a bit of extra protein as a bonus. It's easy to make these nut-free by swapping out the pistachios for shredded coconut. The date mixture will be sticky when you work with it, so greasing your hands with a few drops of coconut oil will make it easier to handle.

MAKES 6 SERVINGS

½ lb (227 g) Medjool dates, pitted and roughly chopped

1 ½ cups (70 g) unsweetened coconut flakes

2 tbsp (12 g) vanilla protein powder

Zest of 1 lemon

1 tbsp (15 mL) lemon juice

¼ tsp sea salt

¼ cup (35 g) pistachios, chopped

Place all the ingredients except the pistachios in a food processor and process until it forms a sticky, cohesive ball. Refrigerate the mixture about 10 minutes so it firms up. Place the chopped pistachios in a separate bowl.

Use about 1 small rounded spoonful of the mixture, and shape it into a ball between your hands. Then roll the balls in the chopped pistachios.

For bars instead of balls, press the mixture into a greased square baking dish, then freeze until solid and cut.

TOTAL RECIPE MACRONUTRIENTS (IN GRAMS PER SERVING)

PROTEIN	2G
FAT	6G
TOTAL CARB	32G
NET CARB	27G

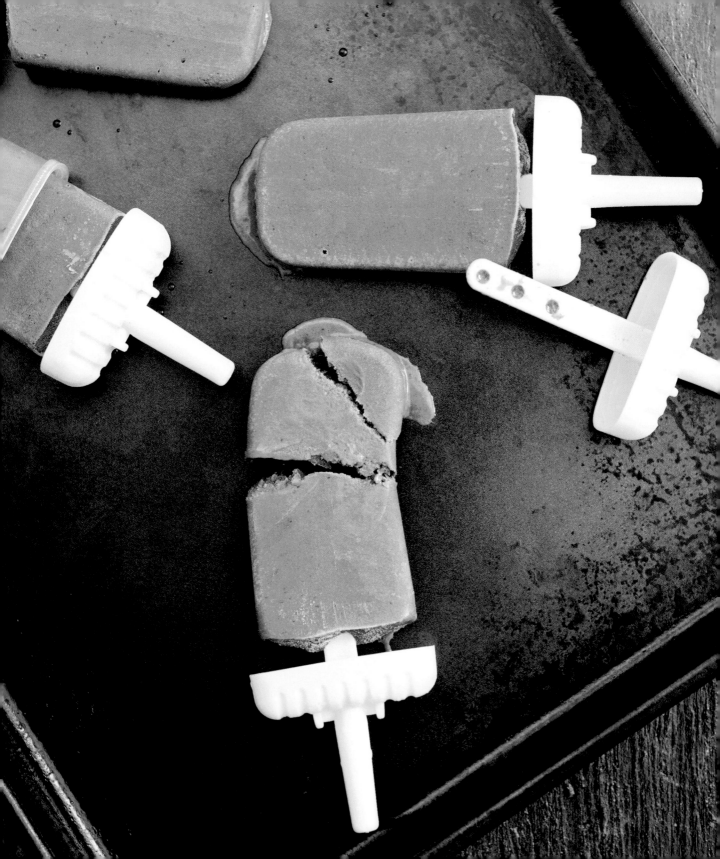

BANANA FUDGESICLES

SIX SIMPLE INGREDIENTS, ONE COOL TREAT

Growing up, Fudgesicles were a favorite summer treat. Us kids would always try to eat up the cool, chocolaty goodness before it melted. I wanted to re-create that experience but with clean ingredients and no extra sugar. Avocado and almond milk are healthy fats, and the dates give a hint of sweetness, especially if your bananas are on the green-tipped side.

MAKES 6 SERVINGS

2 small ripe bananas (10 oz [284 g]), peeled

½ medium avocado (3 oz [85 g]), pitted

1 ¼ cup (296 mL) almond milk

¼ cup (22 g) cocoa powder

2 Medjool dates (38 g), pitted

1 tsp vanilla extract

Place all the ingredients in a high-powered blender or food processor. Blend on high until the mixture is creamy and smooth, about 30 seconds.

Pour the mixture into popsicle molds—my set of six uses about ¼ cup/60 milliliters of liquid in each Popsicle mold—and freeze at least 3 hours or until the pops are solid.

TOTAL RECIPE MACRONUTRIENTS (IN GRAMS PER SERVING)	
PROTEIN	3G
FAT	3G
TOTAL CARB	16G
NET CARB	13G

LEMON VANILLA CUSTARD WITH BLUEBERRY SAUCE

A SIMPLE, YET SATISFYING, TREAT FORTIFIED WITH GUT-HEALING GELATIN

This treat is really nutritious, with coconut milk as a good source of medium chain triglycerides, a fast-burning fat, and gelatin to soothe the gut and joints. The lush blueberry topping is cooked-down fruit, which is rich in antioxidants.

MAKES 4 TO 5 SERVINGS

FOR THE TOPPING

2 cups (150 g) blueberries

2 tbsp (30 mL) water

FOR THE CUSTARD

1 can (14 oz [414 mL]) coconut milk

2 egg yolks

Zest of 2 lemons

3 tbsp (45 mL) lemon juice

2 tbsp (30 mL) honey

1 tsp vanilla extract

1 tbsp (7 g) high-quality grass-fed gelatin

To make the topping, combine the blueberries and water in a small pot over medium-low heat. Cook the blueberries until they pop and become a thick sauce. Refrigerate the sauce to thicken a bit more.

Meanwhile, prepare the custard. In a medium pot, combine the coconut milk, egg yolks, lemon zest, lemon juice and honey. Whisk the ingredients until everything is combined. Cook the mixture for about 5 minutes over medium-low heat until it thickens slightly and coats the back of a spoon. Turn off the heat and whisk in the vanilla extract. While whisking, pour the gelatin into the mixture until it's completely dissolved.

Divide the custard evenly into 4 small ramekins and chill for at least 2 hours or until the custard is set. When you're ready to serve it, spoon some of the blueberry sauce on top.

TOTAL RECIPE MACRONUTRIENTS (IN GRAMS PER SERVING)	
PROTEIN	3G
FAT	14G
TOTAL CARB	20G
NET CARB	17G

BAKED COCONUT CHOCOLATE APPLES

TOTALLY DECADENT WITH JUST FIVE INGREDIENTS

Baked apples are so simple yet satisfying and even, dare I say, a bit decadent? To prep these, I take the cores out of the apples but don't go all the way through—that's key to preventing the coconut butter from leaking out of the bottom. You can make your own coconut butter or, if you're busy, buy it from the market to save time. I always look for a dark chocolate that is free from soy lecithin and at least 80% cocoa.

MAKES 4 SERVINGS

4 firm-fleshed red apples, such as Pink Lady

⅓ cup (73 g) coconut butter

¼ cup (32 g) chopped almonds

¼ cup (32 g) chopped dark chocolate

¼ tsp sea salt

Preheat the oven to 375°F/191°C and have a small baking dish ready. An 8-inch x 8-inch/20-centimeter x 20-centimeter dish or small cast-iron skillet works well.

Using a very sharp paring knife, cut around the core of the apple, making a circle. Don't cut all the way through to the bottom. With a spoon, scoop out the core until you have a hole inside the apple that goes about three-quarters of the way through. In a small bowl, mix the coconut butter, chopped almonds, chocolate and salt. Spoon this mixture into the hollowed-out apples, then place them in the baking dish. Bake the apples, uncovered for about 35 to 40 minutes, or until the apples have softened but aren't mushy.

Try Granny Smith apples for a tarter bite.

TOTAL RECIPE MACRONUTRIENTS (IN GRAMS PER SERVING)	
PROTEIN	2G
FAT	17G
TOTAL CARB	31G
NET CARB	24G

CHAPTER SEVEN

SCRUMPTIOUS SAUCES AND SEASONINGS

Expand your quiver of sauces and seasonings to add simple, nutritious flavor to food. If you find yourself bored with basic meals like meat and veggies, make some sauces to spice things up.

Some of my favorite flavor enhancers and sauce ingredients are healthy fats like olive oil, avocados and nuts. They can add a creamy texture or a crunch, and they punch up the fat profile of meals. Remember, a Paleo template is not low fat. Nutritious sources such as cold-pressed plant oils, high-quality animal fats, avocado, nuts, olives and coconut products are an important part of a healthy diet for performance-minded individuals.

Fats help maintain cellular integrity, form the precursors for hormones, provide energy, assist in the absorption of fat-soluble vitamins and help us feel satiated when we eat.

Of course, spices are another awesome way to bring flavor and life to food. Many, such as turmeric and ginger, are renowned for their ability to fight inflammation and aid recovery.

BLACKENING DUST

ADDS A SPICY KICK TO ANY MEAT

Having a great blackening seasoning in your arsenal of spices is essential. This one builds a ton of flavor with a backbone of smoked paprika and a punch of heat from the cayenne. It doesn't have any salt, though, so be sure to adjust that separately. Sprinkle on chicken before you grill it, or use for Blackened Fish Soft Tacos With Mango Slaw (page 106).

MAKES ¼ CUP (40 G)

1 tbsp (15 g) smoked paprika

1 tbsp (10 g) garlic powder

1 tbsp (7 g) onion powder

½ tbsp (8 g) black pepper

1 tsp dried thyme

¾ tsp cayenne pepper

½ tsp ground coriander

Combine all the ingredients in a small bowl and mix well. Store in an airtight container.

TOTAL RECIPE MACRONUTRIENTS (IN GRAMS PER SERVING)

PROTEIN	TRACE
FAT	TRACE
TOTAL CARB	2G
NET CARB	2G

LEMON ROSEMARY FINISHING SALT

ADDS ZING TO CHICKEN, FISH AND VEGGIES

Finishing salts with herbs and aromatics are gaining popularity as a way to sprinkle on a bit of extra flavor to food once it's cooked. The concept is quite simple: Add lemon zest and chopped rosemary to sea salt, then bake everything on very low heat until everything is dry. This keeps well for a few months.

MAKES ¼ CUP (59 G)

¼ cup (60 g) coarse sea salt

Zest of 2 lemons

½ tbsp (2 g) fresh rosemary, chopped

Preheat the oven to 250°F/93°C. Spread the ingredients on a clean baking sheet and mix them until they're evenly combined. Bake the salt mixture for about 45 minutes, stirring every 15 minutes or so, until the zest and rosemary are dry.

Store in an airtight container.

Use chopped chives instead of rosemary.

TOTAL RECIPE MACRONUTRIENTS (IN GRAMS PER SERVING)	
PROTEIN	TRACE
FAT	TRACE
TOTAL CARB	2G
NET CARB	0G

MINT BASIL BRAZIL NUT PESTO

DAIRY-FREE PESTO WITH TONS OF FLAVOR

Pesto is a classic condiment that a lot of people forgo when they start Paleo because it traditionally contains cheese. Luckily, pesto can be just as tasty when made without dairy. Here I've added mint to freshen the flavor and subbed out pine nuts for Brazil nuts to up the selenium content. Serve over zucchini noodles, eggs, grilled chicken and more. The possibilities are endless!

MAKES 4 SERVINGS

1 cup (16 g) basil leaves, packed

½ cup (8 g) mint leaves, packed

⅓ cup (54 g) unroasted Brazil nuts

¼ cup (59 mL) + 1 tbsp (15 mL) olive oil

1 tbsp (15 mL) lemon juice

1 clove garlic

¼ tsp sea salt

⅛ tsp red pepper flakes

Combine all the ingredients in a food processor or blender and process until smooth.

Keeps for 1 or 2 days in the refrigerator.

TOTAL RECIPE MACRONUTRIENTS (IN GRAMS PER SERVING)	
PROTEIN	2G
FAT	26G
TOTAL CARB	3G
NET CARB	1G

AVOCADO TOMATILLO SALSA

GREEN SALSA WITH A CREAMY TWIST

Salsa verde—green salsa—is a traditional accompaniment made with a base of tomatillos, jalapeño, herbs and spices. It's delicious just like that, but I really love the creaminess from the ripe avocado and the smokiness from roasting the tomatillos and jalapeño first. This goes really well served on the Blackened Fish Soft Tacos With Mango Slaw (page 106) as well as served on eggs or grilled steak.

MAKES 8 TO 10 SERVINGS

1 lb (454 g) tomatillos, husks removed

½ jalapeño pepper

2 medium avocados (10 oz [284 g]), pitted

½ cup (18 g) cilantro leaves, packed

2 tbsp (10 mL) lime juice

1 clove garlic

½ tsp sea salt

Place the tomatillos and jalapeño pepper on a foil-lined baking sheet. Broil on high for 10 to 15 minutes, flipping them over halfway through the cooking time. Remove from the oven and cool.

Add the cooled tomatillos and jalapeño, plus the rest of the ingredients, to a high-powered blender or food processor. Blend until the mixture smooths out or until it's as chunky or smooth as you like it. I like a little texture to mine.

TOTAL RECIPE MACRONUTRIENTS (IN GRAMS PER SERVING)	
PROTEIN	1G
FAT	4G
TOTAL CARB	6G
NET CARB	4G

CREAMY OLIVE OIL MAYO

SIMPLE, CREAMY HOMEMADE MAYONNAISE MADE BETTER WITH OLIVE OIL

For a long time, mayo got a bad rep because store-bought bottles are made with industrial vegetable oils. Maybe it was all the cheap vegetable oil, but when you make your own and use olive oil, you get a creamy spread that adds healthy fat to your dishes. Plain mayo can be jazzed up with spices, herbs and aromatics to make as many different variations as you can dream up. The key to making mayo is to use room temperature ingredients—so they integrate fully into the emulsion—and to pour the oil slowly.

MAKES 1 ¼ CUPS (296 ML)

1 cup (237 mL) + 2 tbsp (30 mL) light-tasting olive oil

1 tbsp (15 mL) lemon juice

½ tsp sea salt

1 large egg

In a blender, combine ¼ cup/59 milliliters olive oil, lemon juice, salt and the egg. Cover the blender and let this mixture come to room temperature for about 30 minutes.

Run the blender on low for about 30 seconds, then remove the insert from the lid and get ready to drizzle the rest of the oil in. You need to pour slowly in a thin stream, and increase the blender speed from low to medium. After some of the oil has been poured in—about half—you'll hear the blender motor change pitch. Keep pouring slowly until the rest of the oil is integrated.

Scoop the mayo into a storage container and mark the egg's expiration date on it: That's when you'll discard any leftover mayo.

To make Garlic Aioli, stir 1 teaspoon Dijon mustard and 4 cloves of finely chopped garlic into the prepared mayo.

TOTAL RECIPE MACRONUTRIENTS (IN GRAMS PER SERVING)

PROTEIN	6G
FAT	248G
TOTAL CARB	2G
NET CARB	2G

SMOKY CHIPOTLE MAYO

A VERSATILE MAYO TOPPING WITH A SPICY KICK

Adding a spicy element to your plate is one simple way to balance the flavors in a dish. This mayo is good on just about everything from steak to eggs, and it's perfect for adding some healthy fat to your meals.

MAKES ½ CUP (118 ML)

½ cup (118 mL) Creamy Olive Oil Mayo (page 206)

½ tsp ground chipotle pepper

⅛ tsp hot sauce

In a small bowl, mix the mayo, chipotle pepper and hot sauce. Stir to combine, and refrigerate until using.

Look for hot sauce with only three ingredients: Chilies, vinegar and salt.

TOTAL RECIPE MACRONUTRIENTS (IN GRAMS PER SERVING)	
PROTEIN	3G
FAT	99G
TOTAL CARB	1G
NET CARB	1G

AWESOMESAUCE

DELICIOUS DIP THAT GOES WITH EVERYTHING

Awesomesauce was inspired by a dip I had at a party. I went on a mission to re-create a version that was still as good and Paleo-friendly to boot. Use this as a dip for raw veggies, sweet potato fries or as a topping for grilled meat.

MAKES 8 SERVINGS

1 cup (146 g) almonds, soaked in water for 24 hours and drained

½ cup (118 mL) water

¼ cup (59 mL) olive oil

¼ cup (59 mL) lemon juice

1 tbsp (15 mL) coconut aminos

½ tbsp garlic powder

½ tbsp nutritional yeast

1 tsp ground chipotle pepper

1 tsp sea salt

¼ tsp cayenne pepper

Combine all the ingredients in a high-powered blender or food processor and blend until smooth.

Substitute cashews for almonds.

TOTAL RECIPE MACRONUTRIENTS (IN GRAMS PER SERVING)	
PROTEIN	4G
FAT	16G
TOTAL CARB	5G
NET CARB	3G

TANGY LEMON DRESSING

A SIMPLE DRESSING TO KEEP IN YOUR REPERTOIRE

Dressings and sauces really punch up the flavor of staple dishes like grilled meat and roasted veggies. If you're a creature of habit, they're a simple way to prevent food boredom and monotony. Salad dressings are usually notorious for artificial ingredients and added sugar, but the good news is you can make your own in just a couple of minutes with some basic ingredients. I always have a few lemons and limes on hand for making my own dressing.

MAKES ¼ CUP (59 ML)

Zest of 1 lemon

2 tbsp (30 mL) lemon juice

⅛ tsp sea salt

Pinch black pepper

2 tbsp (30 mL) olive oil

Place the lemon zest, lemon juice, sea salt and black pepper in a medium bowl and whisk to combine. Then slowly drizzle the olive oil in while constantly whisking.

TOTAL RECIPE MACRONUTRIENTS (IN GRAMS PER SERVING)	
PROTEIN	TRACE
FAT	27G
TOTAL CARB	3G
NET CARB	3G

CREAMY MANGO JALAPEÑO DRESSING

SWEET, TANGY AND A LITTLE BIT SPICY

This dressing was a happy coincidence. When I was developing my Crunchy Slaw With Chicken (page 158), I wanted to add some sweet and spice. Instead of adding chopped mango and jalapeño, I threw it all into the blender and came up with this dressing. It's surprisingly creamy, and you can customize the heat level by keeping more or less of the jalapeño seeds.

MAKES 4 SERVINGS

1 cup (92 g) mango, fresh or frozen

Zest of 1 lime

6 tbsp (90 mL) lime juice

2 tbsp (30 mL) light-tasting olive oil

1 jalapeño pepper, stem removed

½ tsp sea salt

¼ tsp fish sauce

Combine all the ingredients in a high-powered blender or food processor and blend until smooth.

If you add the entire jalapeño pepper—seeds and inner white membrane—the dressing will be medium to spicy.

TOTAL RECIPE MACRONUTRIENTS (IN GRAMS PER SERVING)

PROTEIN	TRACE
FAT	7G
TOTAL CARB	10G
NET CARB	9G

ROASTED POBLANO SAUCE

Poblano peppers are one of my favorites: They're low on the spicy scale and are really flavorful. When charred and blended with homemade mayo, lime and spices, the result is a sauce that's perfect for perking up fish and chicken.

MAKES 4 SERVINGS

1 poblano pepper (2 oz [57 g])

½ cup (118 mL) Creamy Olive Oil Mayo (page 206)

½ tbsp (8 mL) lime juice

⅛ tsp sea salt

⅛ tsp black pepper

⅛ tsp cayenne pepper

Blacken the skin of the poblano pepper by placing it on a foil-lined baking sheet under a broiler set to high. You can also char the outside by holding it over a gas stovetop burner and turning it with metal tongs until the skin bubbles and starts to char. Let the pepper cool, then cut off the stem and slice it open. Scrape out and discard the seeds.

Combine all the ingredients in a high-powered blender or food processor and blend until smooth.

Note the expiration date of the egg you used for the mayo on the container for this recipe, and discard leftovers on that date.

TOTAL RECIPE MACRONUTRIENTS (IN GRAMS PER SERVING)	
PROTEIN	1G
FAT	25G
TOTAL CARB	2G
NET CARB	2G

KICKED UP SRIRACHA

THIS FAMOUS HOT SAUCE GETS A SURPRISING ORANGE TWIST

Sriracha, made famous by the Huy Fong company with a rooster on the bottle, is a versatile sauce that adds heat and spice to any food. I first blogged a sriracha recipe way back in 2011, and since then, I've tweaked and refined the flavor over the years. The result is an orange-kissed but still spicy vibrant red sauce that really does go with everything.

MAKES 1 CUP (237 ML)

½ lb (227 g) red jalapeño peppers, stems removed

¼ cup (59 mL) apple cider vinegar

6 cloves garlic

Zest of 1 orange

Juice of 1 orange

1 tsp fish sauce

1 tsp honey

½ tsp sea salt

Place all the ingredients in a high-powered blender or food processor. Blend until everything is broken down and smooth. Then pour the sauce into a small pot, bring it to a boil and reduce it to a simmer. Cook for about 10 minutes or until the sriracha is reduced in volume by about one-third.

For mild sauce, remove the seeds from all the peppers. For medium, only remove the seeds from half the peppers.

TOTAL RECIPE MACRONUTRIENTS (IN GRAMS PER SERVING)	
PROTEIN	5G
FAT	2G
TOTAL CARB	46G
NET CARB	36G

ACKNOWLEDGMENTS

To the readers—your dedication to sport and the sacrifices you've made for it inspired this book. Providing you with nourishing recipes that support and enhance your performance is my mission. I wish you success in all your endeavors!

To my Z—without your unwavering support and holding lots of black-and-white foam board, this book would have been infinitely harder to make. You've always encouraged me to do the work, pursue virtuosity and answer the hard questions. I'm lucky you are my one.

To my family and friends—when I decided to leave the relative safety of my teaching career, you had my back and pushed me to reach for the stars. I wouldn't be here living my passion without you.

To the Page Street team and family of authors—thank you for welcoming me, putting your faith in my vision and seeing this book to fruition. You've helped produce a fantastic resource for Paleo athletes worldwide.

ABOUT THE AUTHOR

When Steph was a kid, she couldn't decide between being a ballerina or a soccer player, and in fifth grade, her mom made her choose one. Like any good adrenaline junkie, she picked the latter, and so began what's been a lifetime of competitive sports. She's done everything from track to Tae Kwon Do, to almost a decade of racing mountain bikes—complete with her fair share of crashes and bruises. Most recently, she does CrossFit and Olympic weight lifting. Simply put, being an athlete is in her blood.

It wasn't always easy, though. Despite being active, Steph battled with her weight growing up and struggled with erratic blood sugar, digestive problems and endometriosis. She tried everything from Weight Watchers to vegetarianism to get healthy, but no amount of counting points or soy burgers seemed to work. Desperate to feel better, Steph went Paleo in early 2010 after hearing about it from a friend, and immediately experienced the benefits, both in athletic performance and overall health. In an effort to keep track of her favorite recipe creations, she started her blog shortly after. What Steph didn't realize at the time is that the stage was set for a significant life change.

She'd been teaching high school biology and chemistry for nearly a decade when the feeling that it wasn't her lifelong calling started to nag at the back of her mind. Steph knew that her mission was helping people become healthier, happier and harder to kill. She melded her love of competition, her formal education in human physiology and nutrition and her 12 years of teaching experience into Stupid Easy Paleo. In 2013, after a few years of soul-searching, she left the four walls of the classroom to teach people around the world the foundations of whole food, Paleo-based nutrition.

Steph lives—and lifts barbells—in Southern California with her husband Z.

INDEX